THE CHILDREN REMEMBER

STORIES OF MINNESOTA CHILDREN DURING WORLD WAR II

THE CHILDREN
REMEMBER

Stories of Minnesota Children
During World War II

To My Friend in the Lord — Yvonne —

Sharon Eberhardt Schulte

Sharon Eberhardt Schulte

NORTH STAR PRESS OF ST. CLOUD, INC.

St. Cloud, Minnsota

DEDICATION

I dedicate this book to the American children whose lives were over-shadowed by World War II, especially those children who knew the trauma of losing a family member in active duty during World War II.

Published by
North Star Press of St. Cloud, Inc.
P.O. Box 451
St. Cloud, Minnesota 56302
northstarpress.com

TABLE OF CONTENTS

Introduction

My own memory-bank is full of what I experienced as a grade-school child in Minnesota during World War II. Sometimes it seems as if I was on the frontlines when I learned of the deaths of my schoolmates' fathers. I am in my seventies now. About two years ago, I jotted down all of my childhood memories of World War II. I have a story to tell.

For decades I have read the stories of valiant veterans of the war. I have seen the movies. I am aware many veterans choose not to share a word about their hideous war experiences. To those veterans who have stories they want to tell, it is right their stories be told and be told first. I have favorites among the courageous stories they have shared.

There is another segment of Americans who have stories to tell too. That is the Americans who were children during those years. Part of my childhood was lived in the shadow of World War II.

I have lived in Minnesota all of my life and never more than seven miles from my birthplace, St. Cloud. I surely cannot speak for all American children. I can speak for those who were children of the war years who lived in Minnesota, those who I interviewed for this book. It is my belief that similar stories can be told by a portion of children throughout the United States.

As American veterans of World War II are dying rapidly now due to their advanced age, so are the American children of the war who are in their seventies and eighties.

My dad followed the war closely through the newspapers and radio. The war was always the topic of conversation at home, especially when visitors came. As a result I was war-aware at a very young age. Our family aided troops through activities in the community, school, and home. We lived the war everyday on this side of the ocean.

After I completed my own notes on the war, I began to ask family and close friends what they could recall regarding the World War II. I hunted up classmates, and their memories added to my collection and also confirmed what I remembered. I branched out to other people in my age bracket. Many of them said to me, "This is the first time anyone has ever asked me about what I experienced as a child during the war." Others wondered if what they knew about the war really mattered. After all, they were just children, and they bowed to the soldiers who took precedence over themselves. The children too, experienced times of fright and times of victory in the homeland. I must include, too, times of great loss. The children have gone discounted and unrecognized for decades.

For the last two years, I managed to bring every conversation I engaged in around to the war. So many people had stories right on the tips of their tongues. Other people with not such ready memories could be coaxed into remembering if I shared a story or two I already collected. It was like priming the pump. I stood in awe sometimes at what I was hearing as they told how they coped on the home front during their childhood with the pressure war put on them and their families. Some children were emotionally wounded by the war, and there was no medic to rush to help them.

I added their stories to mine. Hear us. These Minnesota children experienced World War II.

1

The First Lady Visits St. Cloud Schools

When the first lady of our land, Eleanor Roosevelt, wife of Franklin Delano Roosevelt, visited St. Cloud, Minnesota, in the fall of 1941, it was a major historical event for the city. She managed to work into her agenda brief visits to many local schools. One of her planned stops was Jefferson Elementary School at Third Avenue and Fifth Street Northeast, two blocks from our home.

In preparation for her visit, the children stood in line on the sidewalk in front of the school, smaller children in front so they could see and be seen. After she exited the car, she walked the entire length of the line, smiling, talking to some and patting a few on their heads. It was exciting for the children and staff.

My older brother, Kenny, who was in the sixth grade, was so impressed to see the president's wife. He was also impressed with the car she rode in, a black Cadillac. He kept repeating to anyone who would listen, "That was the biggest car I ever saw!"

My sisters were breathless with the wonder of it all, to think they saw someone who lived in the White House. They noticed her beautiful

Eleanor Roosevelt visits Jefferson School, St. Cloud, Minnesota, on October 29, 1941. (Photo courtesy of the Stearns History Museum—Myron Hall Photo Collection)

clothing, especially the silver fox fur she wore about her neck. The head was on the fur piece, and some of the smaller children were convinced the eyes of the fox were looking straight at them! It was an awesome day to see Eleanor Roosevelt in person.

Some people in the neighborhood gathered in the park across the street, hoping to get a glimpse of the famous woman. Others waited on the corners to wave as she drove away.

It was exciting for this Central Minnesota town, population 24,170, to host Eleanor Roosevelt. Because of this visit, we felt a special connection always to President and Eleanor Roosevelt.

Eleanor Roosevelt continued her tour of St. Cloud, stopping at Lincoln Elementary. (Photo courtesy of the Stearns History Museum—Myron Hall Photo Collection)

Many of the children seeing Eleanor Roosevelt wore hand-me-down coats and shoes as they gazed upon Mrs. Roosevelt. These children were all born in the years of the Great Depression. World War II was to be declared shortly, following the bombing of Pearl Harbor five weeks later, and they would be living the next nearly four years of their childhood with their country involved in the Great War.

I was a child born in the Depression and in grade school during World War II.

Top is Eleanor Roosevelt's visit to Cathedral High School, and the bottom photo shows Eleanor Roosevelt at St. Anthony's Catholic Grade School. (Photos courtesy of the Stearns History Museum—Myron Hall Photo Collection)

2

The Family Learns of the Bombing of Pearl Harbor

The United States was not on stable ground when Pearl Harbor was bombed by the Japanese. Many American servicemen died in that attack. Our country was still recovering from the stock market crash of 1929, resulting in the Great Depression. In the wake of the crash, families had been struggling to adjust to a new lifestyle, living with less. Now with World War II beginning, we would again be facing new challenges on the home front.

I was a young child living with my family of eight in St. Cloud, Minnesota, in the central part of the state. We lived in a rented house one block east of the Mississippi River and three blocks north of St. Germain Street. We were on the corner of Second Avenue and Third Street Northeast.

Six children were born to our parents, Harley and Sylvia (Genz) Eberhardt, from 1929 to 1940. In birth order we are: Dolores, Kenny, Nita, Verna, Sharon (Me), and Dale.

Our dad was a hard-working man, and he mourned the fact that steady jobs were scarce. He did some seasonal work helping area farmers

The Harley and Sylvia (Genz) Eberhardt Family. Left to right, back row: Kenny, Dad, Mom, Dolores; front row: Dale, Nita, and Sharon (Me). Verna, the fourth-oldest child, is taking the picture. It is Father's Day 1943. (Author's collection)

at harvest time, and during the winter he would harvest ice from the Mississippi for use in home and business ice boxes. There were several granite quarries in the area, and he appreciated the opportunity to haul the completed engraved headstones to cemeteries in Central Minnesota. He set them up on the graves.

Mom and Dad somehow managed to see to it that there was enough cash to pay the landlord, Mr. Keaveny, when he came each month to collect the rent.

Meals were skimpy and with little variety. We ate mostly potatoes because they were cheap, plentiful and filling. Oatmeal and pancakes were often on the menu too. Meat, fresh fruit, and milk seldom found their way to our table. We had canned milk for our cereal. Our grandparents, Herman and Elizabeth (Miller) Genz, brought us eggs from their hobby farm. Taking the edge off our hunger was Mom's greater concern over nutrition. My oldest brother, Kenny, was so hungry for something sweet he took the sugar bowl under the bed, and with a spoon he ate it all. He had been denied so many things, he took matters into his own hands and helped himself to a treat. Mom didn't scold him; she felt badly the situation was such that Kenny had been driven to do this.

It was a treat when the apple trees in our yard produced an abundant harvest every fall. We could eat all we wanted. Mom

Front row: Dale and a counsin, Carol Ness; Back row: Sharon and Verna. Verna was missing from the family picture because she was taking the photo. She is the fourth oldest child in the family. (Author's collection)

should have received an award for all she created with apples. Apple sauce covered our pancakes all winter.

Mom sewed nearly every bit our clothing on her non-electric, foot-pedal-powered treadle sewing machine. The girls always wore dresses. Slacks were men's clothes, we were told. Dad cobbled our shoes on an upside down iron shoe on a stand, to make them last a bit longer. Mom cut all our hair and that of many neighbors too.

Poor didn't mean unhappy. We were creative poor people and invented many ways every day to have fun. The neighbors, the John Alhes family, mirrored ours with more girls than boys. There were other large families on our block too, all living similar lifestyles. Lonliness was something we never experienced. There were always enough kids to play yard games with us. We staged circuses in our yard, doing an assortment of tricks on the apple tree brances. Our part-collie dog, Lassie, became any animal we wanted him to be. We were together, secure, and I knew I was loved every day of my life.

We had eight much-anticipated family celebrations every year—our birthdays. Mom always managed to have on hand enough ingredients to make a huge birthday cake. All these special cakes were baked in the big enamel dishpan. Mom and the older girls were careful not to chip the dishpan when they did dishes each day. A chip would mean the cake would burn in that spot. No birthday was ever forgotten. In the past seventy years, I have never seen a bakery cake as beautiful as our dishpan birthday cakes.

We never had a car until later in the war years. We walked everywhere we went. We didn't have much, our world was small and so safe. There were no locks on the doors, so we never needed a key.

OUR ONE LUXURY

Our family had one luxury and how we appreciated it, especially in the winter. We had a floor-model radio that stood almost three feet high and was eighteen-inches square. When the radio was on, the large dial in the front glowed orange. We would sit on the floor around the radio and laugh at *Fibber McGee and Molly*. When we listened to the mysteries we would huddle together. We had one electric light bulb that hung from the center of the ceiling on a two foot cord. The wood-burning stove was in the center of the room. It was cozy and safe.

On that radio Dad learned that the Japanese had attacked the American military men on Pearl Harbor. This news frightened us, and the following days were somber. Dad kept his ear to the radio for further details. Sometimes there would be so much static he couldn't hear the announcer. I doubt that he ever missed one of President Franklin

Delano Roosevelt's famed Fireside Chats when he kept the American citizens informed about the war. We had rules in the house about the radio. We could be in the living room when Dad listened to the war news, but we couldn't talk. We had to go to the kitchen if we wanted to talk. When static interfered it really frustrated Dad.

Every day I noticed the big black headlines in the local newspaper—more news of the advancing war. Dad would get glum reading the paper sometimes or excited over a victory on the battlefield. He had always been interested in the news from around the world, and now the intensity of his interest piqued our interest in the war. He assured us the war was far away. We would have to travel halfway across the country, then across a wide ocean. The war would never hurt us, he said. He always told the truth, so I believed him. The children in our house knew of World War II from the beginning. We were a war-aware family from the day the Japanese bombed Pearl Harbor.

But allowing children to know about the war was not always the case. My high school friend, Yvonne Eckman Dahm, told me her parents, Oscar and Ruth Eckman, went to great lengths to protect her from knowing anything about World War II. At the time she was their only child and in a lower grade at Roosevelt Elementary school in West St. Cloud. Yvonne had just seen Eleanor Roosevelt at her school. It was an exciting thing to share with her parents. Mrs. Roosevelt said their school was named after "Uncle Teddy Roosevelt." But sharing information about the war with Yvonne was another matter.

If her parents wanted to listen to an upcoming radio news broadcast, they helped her dress in her coat, snow pants, boots, cap, mittens, and scarf and sent her outside to play. They lived at the edge of town, and there weren't neighbors nearby, so she played alone in the snow. When company came to the Eckman home and the war was sure to be the topic of conversation, the adults had to hold back on that discussion until Yvonne was dressed in winter gear and sent out of the house, out of earshot. Visitors came often because they didn't have phones, and they needed to connect with others during home visits. Yvonne clearly

9

remembers three times in one day she was dressed and sent out to play in the cold December weather.

Finally her patents agreed that Yvonne had to be told about the ugly war. Their plan to shield her from it wasn't working very well, and the war was dragging on. There wasn't any counseling at school either. Some adults were so overwhelmed themselves that they didn't know how to explain the war to their little children. I think teachers contended with conflicting concerns of how much the parents wanted their children to know.

BLACKOUTS

Americans learned about blackouts. Instructions were given by the officials to city and rural leaders to schedule blackouts. Residents were instructed to turn off all house lights at a designated time on a certain evening. Street lights, all public lighting, and business lights were to be off too. The purpose of this was to make towns undetectable to possible enemies flying in the area with the intent to bomb American towns. We were told in advance which night this city-wide blackout would take place. At dusk, block wardens with armbands would appear at the neighborhood intersections near our home. When the sirens blew, all the street lights went out, and Dad turned off our house lights. In preparation, we had dragged kitchen chairs into the living room and put them in a circle so we could all hold hands in the dark. From time to time, Dad would go to the window, turn back the edge of the paper shade to see if he could see anything happening. Of course he couldn't; it was too dark.

The eight of us sat in a circle on mismatched chairs and furniture. Dolores held Dale. Dad made Lassie, our "outside" dog, come inside, fearing he would bite the block warden. Lassie knew something was up. He would lie next to Kenny, his body on the floor but his head erect, as were his ears. He was on guard for something. I actually listened for planes.

When the siren sounded the second time, we could turn our house lights on again. I wondered, "If the war was so far away, why were we all hiding in the dark?" Life for us went on, but not as usual, after World War II began.

BLACKOUTS IN SOME RURAL AREAS OF MINNESOTA

People who lived in the country had other things to deal with during the blackouts. Inez Kronenberg, a high school classmate of mine, lived in St. Augusta, just south of St. Cloud. Her parents were Barney and Crescentia Hurrle Kronenberg. She told of having a cupola on the very top of their two-story farm home with an attic on the third floor. On the roof above the attic was a square, fenced-in area. In all the years Inez lived in that house, she never went on the roof in the cupola. Before the blackout started, men, with the permission of her father, would climb to the roof where they could see for miles and keep an eye on the area during the blackout. If cars were moving and had headlights on, the watchmen would take notice, watching into which driveways the cars turned. They would talk to them later about not following blackout procedures.

Patricia Fordyce Young lived in Akeley, Minnesota, during this time, and she related the difficulty farmers had with blackouts. They could hardly stop milking even if it was during the time allotted for blackouts. Cows simply had to be milked. Farmers had to find ways to block the barn windows so no light would leak from them. They had vital work to do, and they had to do it as well as satisfy the black-out rules.

Jefferson Elementary School, Third Avenue and Fifth Street Northeast, St. Cloud, Minnesota, built about 1930. (Photo courtesy of the Stearns History Museum)

3

Learning War-Survival Skills at School

Jefferson Elementary school, where my siblings and I attended, was two blocks from home, down the alley and across the park. I was proud to follow my older sisters and brother to school. I loved school, and I had the same teachers that my older siblings had previously. School was a safe place for me, like home.

I was shocked one day when my teacher announced that we would be having an air-raid warning at school that morning. "If the 'Japs' come to bomb our town and our school, we have to know where to hide," the teacher said. She explained how we already knew what a fire drill was all about. And air-raid warning was like that. When the fire bell sounded, we had to line up and march quickly to a specific, outside location. The warning would sound different than the fire bell, more of a grinding sound. We were to line up and march quickly to the basement. The lower grades were instructed to crawl under the long tables against an inside wall. The older students would be in the gym or in the upstairs hallway. We did as we were instructed when the grinding sound started. I scrambled under the big table and sat behind my friend Norma Wicktor with Timothy Ahles on one side of me and Kenneth Raden on the other. I was afraid and wondered if they were too. I shut my eyes tight so the tears couldn't get out. I was confused. My dad had said the war was far far away and wouldn't hurt us, but my teacher was telling us where to hide from Japanese bombs. Someone was lying, and I didn't know who.

I opened one eye and could see my brother and sister in the gym where it was lighter by the windows. I wanted to be with them. A friend, Darlene Daniels Dols, recently told me that tumbling mats were hauled to the upstairs hallway to be used to protect children crouched there from flying glass. Not all the students fit into the basement. I'm not the only one who remembers the seriousness of the school air-raid warnings.

When the bell rang a second time, the drill was over, and our teacher told us we could put our wraps on and go outside for recess. In Minnesota in the winter some of the playground equipment was put into storage. It wasn't safe to swing on ice-coated swing seats holding onto icy chains. We had to stay away from ice-coated slides. Most of the kids chased each other around on the snowy playground. Some of us couldn't quickly make the transition from hiding from the enemy in the dark basement to playing on the bright playground.

Instead we stood by the fence and poked our mittened hands in and out of the fence squares and talked about the war. We kept watching the skies for Japanese planes, wondering if we could hear the air-raid warning outside. We knew some planes were ours, and we didn't have to be fearful of those. We made up some childish things—we decided Japanese planes were yellow, and we needed to head for cover only if we spotted a yellow plane. During the summer for the next few years if I was outside and saw a plane, I hid in a thicket of lilac bushes if I was in the backyard. If I was in the front, I hid under the porch. In the winter I sought safety in our snow forts. At night I hid under the covers and hoped for the best.

I never heard anyone tell my dad he was wrong about anything. He said the war would never hurt us, and I didn't dare challenged him. If I told the teacher she was wrong, she would send me to the principal's office. But, if the war was far away, why were we hiding in the dark at home and under the basement tables at school? I asked my oldest sister, Dolores, if I should believe dad or the teacher. She said the teacher was right. Dad was trying to protect us from being worried and afraid. Dad was just being dad. He felt better when he thought we weren't afraid. I believed Dolores and the teacher. I would not let Dad know I was afraid.

My friend, Yvonne, at Roosevelt school in west St. Cloud, remembered the air raid warnings at her school. When the warning whistle blew, the students had to go to what she described as a sub-basement with a dirt floor. It was cold in that space. The lighting was poor, and she was afraid. The children were instructed to sit on the floor, crawl under the desks in storage if they could. She hesitated. She had worn a dress and long white stockings, but she followed the orders and sat on the floor. She would have to explain about the dirt on her clothes to her mother when she got home. It was cold sitting on the ground in the winter in Minnesota, especially in a dress. She was anxious for the whistle to blow a second time so she could get out of there. She dreaded air raid warnings.

UNITED STATES OF AMERICA

War Ration Book One

WARNING

1 Punishments ranging as high as *Ten Years' Imprisonment or $10,000 Fine, or Both,* may be imposed under United States Statutes for violations thereof arising out of infractions of Rationing Orders and Regulations.

2 This book must not be transferred. It must be held and used only by or on behalf of the person to whom it has been issued, and anyone presenting it thereby represents to the Office of Price Administration, an agency of the United States Government, that it is being so held and so used. For any misuse of this book it may be taken from the holder by the Office of Price Administration.

3 In the event either of the departure from the United States of the person to whom this book is issued, or his or her death, the book must be surrendered in accordance with the Regulations.

4 Any person finding a lost book must deliver it promptly to the nearest Ration Board.

OFFICE OF PRICE ADMINISTRATION

N° 56759 -141

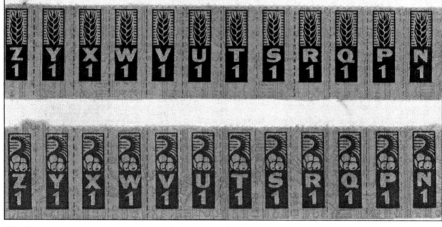

The federal government controlled the nation's food supply by issuing ration stamps to all citizens. Only a limited amount of some food and non-food items were allowed. The purpose was to be able to meet the needs of the American servicemen during World War II.

4

Time to Tighten Our Belts

The war was expanding on many fronts, and thousands of American men and women were going into military service. It was crucial the military have enough food, clothing, and equipment. Word came to American families from the government to "tighten our belts" so there would be enough staples to meet the needs of the armed forces. The United States citizens were encouraged to use less of all commodities to keep the armed forces supplied. Our family couldn't comply with the order exactly; we were on the edge of not having enough as it was.

A school friend, Sibyl Stark Pelz, told me that, at the time of this government request, their family's meticulous record showed that her father, Fred Stark, was making ten dollars a week at the potato warehouse Sauk Rapids. That money had to support their family of three—his wife, Clara Eiffert Stark, Sibyl, and himself. They had a bare-bones existence too. We were compliant families in most regards, but we were unable to comply with this request

RATIONING

We were about to become acquainted with a new government program called "rationing." The federal government was going to control how much

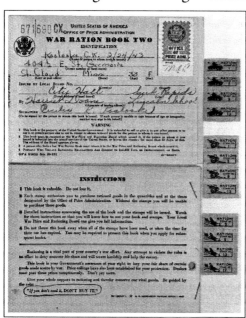

each American could purchase of those things vital to the war effort. The first limits were on food, such as sugar, coffee, and meat. Non-food items were soon limited as well. The military's need for leather for boots was staggering. We were allotted a specific number of pairs of shoes. That was not a hardship for us. We, like many American families, were accustomed to wearing hand-me-down shoes. Style wasn't a consideration. If the shoes were long enough, they were good enough. We didn't have a car when the war began, so the rationing of gas and tires wasn't a concern to us.

Using the ration books widely was a daily aspect of the war. These books carried a warning of imprisonment for misusing the stamps. Rationing was serious business.

In the spring of 1942, mom received eight rationing books, one for each member of the family. I remember handling my book with my name on it. Mom took it back from me in a hurry. She had to shop carefully. She planned to save as much sugar as she could from each of our allotments for the canning season.

VICTORY GARDENS

The federal government also urged Americans to plant a vegetable garden or increase the size of their garden if they already had one. Food was going to be scarce if Americans didn't rally to the call. Families needed to produce their own food so there would be more on the commercial market for the military. Now we could fit into the new plan.

We had a large corner lot with no garage. Our garden was good sized. Dad asked the landlord, Mr. Keaveny, if he could till up even more of the yard so we could plant a "Victory" garden, as the new war-time garden plan was called. Mr. Keaveny granted the permission. Dad hired a man, Lee Burnett, who lived near the Benton County Fairgrounds to come with his team of horses. The neighborhood children came to watch as Burnett and his team of horses turned the ground.

The government initiated this Victory Garden project, and it was encouraged through schools. Some seeds were even distributed at school. I can remember we bought seeds labeled with "Victory Garden Seeds" on the packages. We could earn a lapel pin in the shape of a "V" for working in our Victory Garden. We pulled weeds and picked potato bugs for hours on end, knowing all our work would result in more food for the soldiers.

My local dentist, Dr. Greg Pappenfus whose childhood home was near Wilson School on St. Cloud's north side, told me his family owned a vacant lot next door. His father made the lot into a Victory Garden from the sidewalk to the alley. He said keeping the huge garden weeded to please his fastidious father was a lot of work. The garden produced enough vegetables to last his family for a year. He had ingenious ways to preserve the produce. The extra food was given away to military families.

A couple years later, we moved eight blocks away to another rented house on the corner of Wilson Avenue and Fouth Street Southeast, near Lincoln School. The new landlord, Mr. Grams, lived across the Mississippi River on St. Cloud's south side. I remember going with mom on the city bus to pay the cash rent when it was due. Mr. Grams was friendly.

There was a garden plot on our new property. Mom asked Mr. Grams if we could plow another portion of the lot for a bigger Victory Garden. We were determined to tighten our belts and not take food that the soldiers needed. Mr. Grams thought our plan was a good idea. Lee Burnett was hired again to turn the grassy area into a garden. Now we had Victory Gardens on both sides of the path to the outhouse.

Yes, we had an in-town outhouse. There were just a few others on our alley. It was embarrassing to trot to the outhouse with the neighbors able to see us. Our corner lot on Wilson Avenue was on the bus route with much passing traffic—more to see us use the outhouse.

Families we knew responded powerfully to any suggested government project we could do on the home front to help with the war. Dad and Mom were proud to go to great lengths to grow our family's food supply. Dad was working more now, and we could buy more things we needed to garden. As young children, we understood why we had to work hard in the garden. We wanted the soldiers to eat well, didn't we?

Young girls were taught how to preserve the vegetables grown in the Victory Gardens. (Photo courtesy the Stearns History Center - Myron Hall Photo Collection)

5

Seeing Adolph Hitler in the Newsreels

O ccasionally during the summer, mom would allow me to go to a Sunday matinee with my four older siblings. The movies cost ten cents plus a two-cent luxury tax. Popcorn was a nickel, and we had to share a couple of boxes. As we walked to the theatre, I'd either run ahead or lagged behind them. The movie theatres were all in the downtown area, so we had to walk across the Mississippi River bridge which was about a city block long and fifty feet above the water. The wooden deck was icy in the winter, and the wind blew bitterly cold. That was why I couldn't go to the movies in the winter. In the summer, we'd pick up rocks at the end of the bridge and threw them in about half way across to watch them splash. Crossing the bridge was an adventure in itself for us. Kenny could throw rocks farther than any of us. I always ran fast past the first building on the west side of the bridge. It was the Tschumperlin funeral home, and kids had told me it was haunted. They liked to scare me.

The first thing shown in the theatre was the newsreel. That was scary too. I saw Adolph Hitler and heard him speak in German. I knew he was in charge of enemy soldiers. I often saw his pictures in the newspapers, so I recognized him, but hearing him speak was different and way more frightening. I saw him with his marching troops. I recalled his men doing the goose step march in a parade with stiff knees as they yelled, "Heil Hitler," with their arms extended in salute. The time of fright passed as the movie started, but I would recall it later and dwell on it.

As children, we sometimes mimicked what we saw. Marge Waldorf Skelton told me her mother, Erma Waldorf, gave her chalk to draw a hopscotch on the sidewalk. When she and her friends would tire of hopscotch, they drew swastikas. They had seen swastikas and knew they had something to do with the war. They were hard to draw and had to be practiced many times before they got one right. No one ever told them they shouldn't do that. Eventually rain washed away the swastikas, but they would draw them all over again.

Some of the neighborhood boys quit playing cowboys and Indians and played American soldiers versus Japanese soldiers or American soldiers against the Germans. I saw an older brother marching his little brother around the park while he pinched his ear and shouted, "Macht schnell" (March fast), German words he'd picked up from newsreels at the movies.

We imitated what we saw and heard. For example, once I was determined to walk the entire length of the bridge doing the German army goose step, never bending my knees, just like I had just seen in the newsreels. Periodically the older kids would look back at me and say over their shoulder, "Stop that!" But I'd set a goal to do it. I remember my legs ached when I finally reached the other side.

I was maturing as the war years were passing. I learned the names and faces of world leaders. I could picture Winston Churchill when I heard him talk on the radio. I knew the radio announcers like H.V. Kaltenborn (Hans von Kaltenborn), Edward R. Murrow, and Cedric Adams. I recognized their voices, but I don't recall seeing pictures of them. Dad had the radio on news broadcasts all the time. I heard the names of many countries, but we didn't have a globe, so I couldn't look them up. It was Hitler's face with his odd square mustache and German speech that I never failed to identify.

Free movie tickets were given to children who had purchased a war bond. The movie was *Snow White and the Seven Dwarfs*. (Photo courtesy the Stearns History Center - Myron Hall Photo Collection)

Worrying about our town being bombed never left me. The neighbor girl, Darlene Daniels Dols, told me she kept a bedroll handy like she saw refugees carry in the newsreels. If she had to leave home in a hurry she was ready. I often thought, "If the enemy bombed our bridge, how would we get down town?"

Signs in a store window on West St. Germain near the Paramount Theatre in downtown St. Cloud could easily be read by children. It was common to see statements like these in magazines, newspapers, matchbook covers, and on billboards. (Photo courtesy the Stearns History Museum - Myron Hall Photo Collection)

The signs read:

With this key Hitler	I am Drafted	I have a score to
closed this door	Store Closed	settle with Hitler
With my shovel	Will Re-Open on	and Tojo first
I'll dig his grave	the day of	Sell Furniture later!
	Hitler's Funeral	

6

Service Stars in the Windows

Whenever I was walking in St. Cloud's downtown area with Mom or my sisters I always insisted that we stop at the Greyhound bus depot. It was just a block from the bridge on St. Germain Street. During the war years, this was an extremely busy place with servicemen passing through town. Soldiers and sailors with their duffle bags sometimes sat outside the building in the sunshine while they waited for a transfer bus. I always looked in the huge window of the bus depot to see more military men sitting on the wooden benches and sometimes sleeping on them. I figured they were all going off to war someplace. The Greyhound buses took them to ships or planes, and they went to war. I shielded my eyes from the light behind so I could get a good look at the young men soon to be on the battlefield. Maybe I would even see them in the newsreels. Whoever was with me would occasionally walk through the depot with me, in the St. Germain Street door and out the other far door onto Fifth Avenue. They wouldn't let me linger long. Now I knew for sure the war was real. I saw real soldiers traveling to get there. Besides parades, the depot was the only place I saw service men.

To this day I regard the old Greyhound bus depot as a historic place of interest, a landmark, even though it has been an appliance store for decades. It is scheduled to be demolished soon.

STARS IN THE WINDOWS

I noticed a couple homes we walked past had flags with blue stars hanging in the front windows. I asked Mom if we could get one for our house. She told me each house with a starred flag in the window meant they had someone in their family in the military service. We couldn't have any because my dad was not a soldier, and my brother was only thirteen.

I was absolutely infatuated by the window flags. They marked the homes soldiers were fighting for was my thought. The number of stars on the flag told how many from that family were in military service. The fringe on the bottom was either blue or gold. Those with a gold star on it meant that a soldier from that house had died in the war.

Mom gave me permission to walk several blocks near our house on my hunt for military service flags in windows. I took my Big Chief tablet with me and wrote down the house number of each place displaying a flag and drew the number of stars they had following the house number.

Later in the war years, after we moved to southeast St. Cloud, I saw a gold star in a window. I ran all the way home to tell Mom. I told her people must be crying in that house. Dad said the war was far away, and it wouldn't hurt us. But we had new neighbors who were hurting.

I was allowed to go one block to Riverside Drive Southeast in the 300 block to search for more star flags, but it was different on Riverside. The houses were big and set back far from the sidewalk. The flags were not so easy to see. If my older sister Verna accompanied me on my star walk I could go further from home.

One day Verna and I found a house very close to the sidewalk on another block with a flag with three stars. I opened my Big Chief tablet to mark down the first house I'd seen with three stars. I noticed that the house didn't have a front door. I pictured all the soldiers coming out the side door wearing their soldier clothing, walking down the sidewalk, crossing over the Mississippi River bridge to get to the Greyhound bus depot to go to war together.

Verna was impatient with me because I was taking so long. She said it wasn't polite to "gawk." Three stars! Three brothers! I couldn't help but gawk!

I often seemed to plant myself in front of that house and

This is one kind of window service flag.

This unidentified somber couple is holding a three-star service flag. (Photo courtesy of the Stearns History Museum - Myron Hall Photo Collection)

wonder about the family. What was it like to have three people missing from the family? What was it like to have three people missing from the supper table? Around our table, we had four wooden chairs and two benches for the eight of us. The highest bench was for the little kids. When one was missing at supper it seemed empty at the table. It must be awfully lonely to have three empty places.

Sometimes on summer afternoons, Mom would take my little brother Dale and me on the city bus to visit her aunt on the west side of the Mississippi near Tech High School. When we were going up the walkway to her house, I got very excited because she had a flag with a star in her window. I never saw a star flag from inside a home. When Mom, her aunt and Dale went into the kitchen for coffee and cookies, I managed to insert myself between the lace curtain and the window flag. I felt the fringe and touched the star. I got my face close to the window and waited for someone to come by and see the flag so they would see me too. I was proud and smiling. I waited as long as I dared, but no one passed by the house. I knew I better get to the kitchen. I didn't think it was okay to be behind the curtain. On a lace doily with a ruffle, mom's aunt had set a picture of a man in a soldier suit. I asked my great aunt about him, and she said it was her son and he was in France.

It was a good day, and I was happy that I was able to touch a flag and star. On the bus ride home I pressed my nose against the window and counted the stars in the windows. I was going to find France on the globe when I got back to school.

TWO SCHOOL MATES' FATHERS KILLED IN ACTION

One day I heard the wailing of a child down the hall from my classroom in Jefferson school. I never heard such crying in all my life. It was so loud. I can almost hear it again as I write this. It didn't stop, and it got even louder. We were all looking at each other around the room. I felt like crying too. Before long we saw "Charolette" walk past our classroom door with two adults. Her crying continued. It got dimmer as they went down the flight of stairs and out the front door. We learned at recess that her dad had been killed in the war. I didn't like to hear such a sad thing when I was away from Mom. After school I got between my two sisters, and we held hands tightly and ran across the park and down the alley to our home to tell Mom the sad news.

The next year Principal Regina Martini came into my sister's classroom and escorted our distant cousin, Jim Upson, to her office. His father had been killed in Europe. Shortly after that, his family moved away, and we rarely saw him. His father, Wells Upson, was buried at the Fort Snelling National Cemetery in Minneapolis.

One day when Charolette was back in school, we were double jumping rope. Two girls were turning the long rope, and Charolette and I were jumping and saying one of those sing-song verses. I was thinking about her dad being gone. I was wondering if there was a flag with a gold star in the window at her house. They lived way across Highway 10, so I would never be able to walk that far from home to see it for myself. My dad would be home for supper; her dad would never again be home for supper. I felt sad. I managed to jump out of the turning rope without missing and without making her miss. I ran to the shady side of the school and cried. World War II had taught me the permanence of death.

Pat Fordyce Young remembered from her childhood in Akely, Minnesota, a family she knew that didn't have a flag for their window, even though they had a son in the service and wanted to honor him. When a picture of a star flag was published in a magazine, the mother cut it out, put it in a frame and hung it on the living room wall.

I do not know if the flags families put in their windows were puchased by the families or given to them by the government. I do know I saw different styles of flags in many home windows.

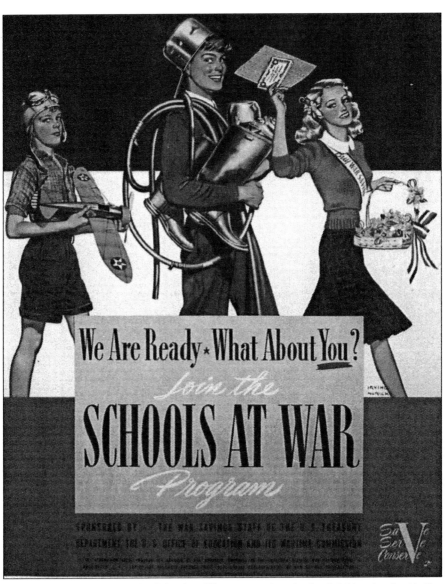

The government sponsored the Schools at War program to get school children involved in the war effort. This flag was displayed at schools. Each child shown represents a way to help the military. The girl has war stamps and bonds. One boy has collected metal and rubber. The other boy has a plane in hand, representing plane spotting.

7

Schools at War

American citizens were encouraged by the federal government to purchase war stamps and war bonds to help fund the war. The government-sponsored program was devoted to getting children involved too.

Through the schools, children could buy war stamps for ten cents each. At Jefferson school we ordered and paid for the stamps early in the week, and on Friday the stamps were delivered to our school. Some kids never had any money for stamps, but most just bought one and a few were able to get a whole dollar's worth at one time.

We were given individual stamp books, which we brought to school every Friday to paste our new stamps in it so we wouldn't lose them.

Every Friday the teachers made a big ceremony of our receiving our stamps. We gathered in the gym where a few children held flags and came forward class by class to receive our stamps. First we said the Pledge of Allegiance. Then, with much gusto, we sang patriotic songs one after another until everyone had received their stamps. We were lusty singers. A song was written to prompt people to buy stamps. I remember it to be:

Buy Bonds. Buy More Bonds and
Send thousands of Jeeps over the sea.

Recently at a women's meeting, I brought up World War II and the buying of stamps at school. I took the liberty to sing the verse of the song above. Before I finished it, one lady joined in and knew the next lines, which I didn't remember. She alone sang the rest of the song. How is it we can remember a sixty-seven-year-old song? As children we were made to feel a very vital part of the war effort.

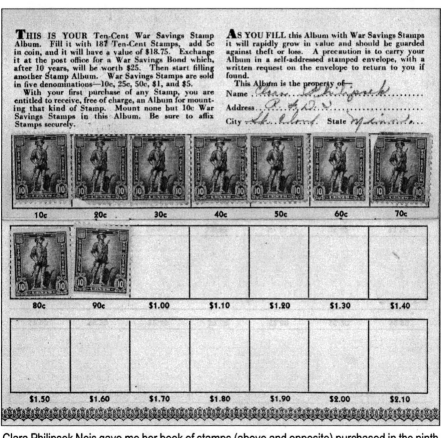

THIS IS YOUR Ten-Cent War Savings Stamp Album. Fill it with 187 Ten-Cent Stamps, add 5c in coin, and it will have a value of $18.75. Exchange it at the post office for a War Savings Bond which, after 10 years, will be worth $25. Then start filling another Stamp Album. War Savings Stamps are sold in five denominations—10c, 25c, 50c, $1, and $5.

With your first purchase of any Stamp, you are entitled to receive, free of charge, an Album for mounting that kind of Stamp. Mount none but 10c War Savings Stamps in this Album. Be sure to affix Stamps securely.

AS YOU FILL this Album with War Savings Stamps it will rapidly grow in value and should be guarded against theft or loss. A precaution is to carry your Album in a self-addressed stamped envelope, with a written request on the envelope to return to you if found.

This Album is the property of
Name
Address
City State

10c   20c   30c   40c   50c   60c   70c

80c   90c $1.00 $1.10 $1.20 $1.30 $1.40

$1.50 $1.60 $1.70 $1.80 $1.90 $2.00 $2.10

Clara Philipsek Neis gave me her book of stamps (above and opposite) purchased in the ninth grade in the St. Cloud public school system.

Children learn to raise a second flag, one with the image from the war stamps booklets. Above is McKinley School in Waite Park, Minnesota. Below is unidentified. (Photos courtesy the Stearns County Museum - Myron Hall Photo Collection)

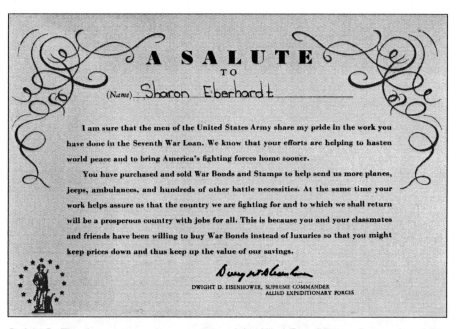

A SALUTE
TO

(*Name*) Sharon Eberhardt

I am sure that the men of the United States Army share my pride in the work you have done in the Seventh War Loan. We know that your efforts are helping to hasten world peace and to bring America's fighting forces home sooner.

You have purchased and sold War Bonds and Stamps to help send us more planes, jeeps, ambulances, and hundreds of other battle necessities. At the same time your work helps assure us that the country we are fighting for and to which we shall return will be a prosperous country with jobs for all. This is because you and your classmates and friends have been willing to buy War Bonds instead of luxuries so that you might keep prices down and thus keep up the value of our savings.

DWIGHT D. EISENHOWER, SUPREME COMMANDER
ALLIED EXPEDITIONARY FORCES

Dwight D. Eisenhower, supreme commander of the Allied Expeditionary Forces signed this document given to school children who helped in the war effort by buying war stamps and bonds.

Students from Lincolhn Elementary School, 306 Fifth Avenue Southeast, St. Cloud, Minnesota, celebrate a war-time victory, March 1945. (Photo courtesy the Stearns County Museum - Myron Hall Photo Collection)

8

Lincoln School Students Celebrate

In the spring of 1945, the children of Lincoln Elementary in southeast St. Cloud, lined up on East St. Germain. They were celebrating because they had brought enough dimes to school to purchase from the Federal Government enough war stamps and bonds to buy not one, but two military jeeps. The children understood their money would be used to buy equipment for the soldiers who were fighting in the war.

In a relatively short time the children had raised enough to buy a jeep, but their efforts didn't stop. They continued buying war stamps until they had accumulated enough to buy two jeeps.

Principal Hulda Liljedahl (also the sixth grade teacher), organized the parade. She wanted her kindergarten through sixth grade children to be recognized for the good they had done in supporting the war effort. A police squad car led the parade, its lights flashing, followed by the school-patrol boys escorting the youthful marchers down the streets. Many of the children carried flags. A banner near the front displayed an enlarged version of the war stamp, a soldier with a gun encircled by stars. They also carried the Schools at War flag.

One hand-painted sign said, "WE DID IT AGAIN." A sign further back said, "2 JEEPS." One young marcher, Beverly Kosloske (DeBode), told me she remembered some of the boys carried toy jeeps.

The parade marched from Fifth Avenue onto Wilson Avenue passed St. Augustine's Catholic church. Spectators along the way removed their hats and saluted the flags the children carried. At the corner of the Ace Bar and Café, they turned left onto East St. Germain Street. They came to Carl's Grocery store owned by Carl and Cecilia "Ducky" Kosloske. Their daughter, Beverly, was in the parade. Carl and Ducky came out to view the parade. One of Carl's butchers joined the military service and was killed in action. The new butcher came out, removed his butcher hat and saluted the flags.

People came out of business places across the street, Mac's Drug Store, Pat Meagher's gas station and the Calvary Baptist church, to view the parade. This was small-town America doing its part in the big war.

The children turned left onto Fourth Avenue Southeast and passed a third church, Salem Lutheran, under the pastorate of Reverend Arthur Chell, whose son, Teddy, was one of the marchers in the parade.

I was not yet attending Lincoln school, so I was not part of the parade.

It would not be unrealistic to say that many of the children marching in the parade were on the receiving end of hugs from family members who were leaving home to enter the military service. The children knew about bombings in far away countries and blackouts in their own neighborhoods. Their relatives could have been on the ships, flying the planes or serving under General Patton in Europe. It was their relatives they wanted to be driving the jeeps they had bought with their dimes.

9

Victory Scrap Iron Drives

As the war raged on so many fronts, the military had an ever-increasing need for iron.

Again the government turned to the citizens for help. The people were asked to donate their scrap iron to be recycled and made into military equipment for war.

In St. Cloud, specific Sundays were designated for the Victory Scrap Iron drives. Residents were encouraged to put their scrap iron on their curbs, and a crew with a truck would come by in the afternoon to pick it up.

As a child, this was an exciting day. Along with some of the neighbor kids I would run around some blocks to see who had the biggest pile. We wondered how many bullets each pile would make. From the bigger piles, we determined they would make those huge cannon-sized balls shot from battleships.

The scrap drives brought the neighbors out, and they stood in clusters up and down the block mostly discussing the war. It was a patriotic thing to do, to donate this iron when it could be sold for cash at the junk yard. It was a sacrifice made knowing it would benefit the military and maybe hasten an end to the war.

My dad seemed to contribute something to every drive. I wanted so much to be part of this, I would go to houses that didn't have a pile on the curb to ask them if they had something little they would like to donate to our pile. Jenny Holstrom, the neighborhood Grandma, never let me down. Once she gave me a coal scuttle, at least that was what dad said it was. It was a round pail with a large spout used for pouring coal into a heating stove. It really added to my pile. The bottom was about rotted through, but it looked big on my pile. One guy across the alley never let me down either. He was in a wheelchair on his back porch, and he'd point to something in his shed he could spare. I would climb around the shed and find it, thank him and run.

During the war we had scrap iron drives on designated Sundays in St. Cloud, the recycled scrap to be used to make military equipment. One unidentified man has on a shirt and tie, which makes me think it is Sunday. The other looks proud of the big donation he has to give. The car in the background is a 1941 Chevrolet, which puts this in the right time period. We all believed that victory had to be just ahead with so much citizen cooperation. (Author's photos)

As I waited for the truck to come, I continued to plead with the neighbors for more scrap iron. I was bold enough to ask the richest man in the neighborhood, and he gave me a handful of stuff. I didn't know what it was, but it was iron and heavy and would make good bullets. I figured rich people didn't have very much junk, but they wanted the war to stop too. After I thanked him, I ran home and added it to our collection. All this made me feel good about helping the soldiers.

We saved our tin cans at home, rinsed them out and squashed them flat, put them in paper sacks and saved them for the scrap drives. Some kids picked up nails wherever they could find them, knowing they were good for the iron drive. It seems like nothing iron escaped our young eyes.

Andy Virden, a retired businessman from Waite Park, Minnesota, told me he remembered climbing on an old cannon that was in the McKinley Elementary schoolyard. He thought it was from the Civil War. The school kids had fun playing on the retired piece of military equipment. But the cannon was donated to the scrap drive and towed away. Maybe the relic from another war, melted down to make arms for the current soldiers helped win World War II. Andy was a young teenager when the cannon was towed out-of-town.

RUBBER DRIVES

Rubber was another commodity in short supply. The United States no longer had access to the rubber suppliers in a foreign lands. To help supply the army, a call went out to the citizens to donate used rubber products. In particular they wanted used tires, rain coats, rubber boots, hoses, and even bathing caps. I remember only a few rubber drives. Mostly people were encouraged to take their rubber donations to collection sites. Children were encouraged to be part of this drive too.

Darlene Daniels Dols, who lived in our neighborhood as a child in the 1940s, told me of her experience with the rubber drive as a child. She had a rubber Betsy Wetsy doll. Darlene was young and loved her doll even if the head didn't stay on very well. Her parents tried to convince her it would be good to donate the broken doll to the rubber drive. Darlene believed it could be fixed. No one agreed with her. Reluctantly she added her doll to the rubber scrap drive. She has some regrets yet for having given up her doll.

Another rubber doll was kept in the family by a younger sister. One day she dug it out and saw that time had eaten a black hole in the body of her rubber doll. Darlene knows her Betsy Wetsy probably would have deteriorated by now. She also knows her heart was not in favor of sacrificing the doll for the war effort. Still, she gave.

NOTHING LEFT TO GIVE

Farmers were very much involved in giving to the scrap drives, but trucks didn't make the rounds to farms to pick up donations. Farmers were expected to haul their contributions to collection sites like a schoolyard, town hall, or county courthouse.

A farm couple and their twelve- and thirteen-year-old sons worked together to load up their trailer with iron for the collection center. Two older sons were already in the military, and their family was generous in their giving to supply their sons in battle. They gave away many things they could still have used, but there was an enemy to defeat. The trailer was way overloaded, and the tires weren't all that good. It was a concern they might not make it all the way to the drop-off site.

As the trailer was being towed towards the lane, the lady remembered some old horseshoes in the shed. She told the boys to run to the shed to get them and then run down the lane to catch up with the trailer and toss them on the heap of iron.

She stood watching the truck and trailer as it turned onto the country road. She thought, *We will win the war. We gave our all, we have nothing left to give.* The sons of the family were in the thick of battle on foreign soil, in countries their family never knew existed before the war started.

The family was eating less purchased food, driving less, wearing their shoes until the soles were paper thin. They were trying to conserve energy by using less electricity. The lights in the house and barn were dimmed all the time. They had nothing left to give. She told how she said aloud, standing in the driveway, "We have nothing left to give. We are going to win this war. We will win this war."

AND WE DID!

Not only were the troops committed, I saw the majority of folk in our area committed—the old and the young.

These unidentified children are shown with a load of newspapers that will be donated to the paper drive. Girls wearing helmets and carrying guns are in the background. (Courtesy of the Stearns County Museum - Myron Hall Photo Collection)

Milkweed growing wild in Sherburne county. (Author's photos)

10

Collecting Milkweed Pods for the Military

I lived in the city during the war years and was well-aware of what city children were doing to help supply American servicemen. Since starting this book, I learned of a huge project rural children did to save lives of the men in the Navy and other branches of service. When I was driving to the Twin Cities recently with my friend Pat Rothstein Dullinger, I asked her what she remembered about World War II. The Rothstein family lived in the country near Rockville, Minnesota, and she told me she picked milkweed pods. When I asked my former high school mate, Inez Kronenberg, she told me the same thing. Living near the farming community of St. Augusta, Minnesota, she and her younger siblings would walk along roads and look for milkweed pods in the ditches. They took bags along to carry the picked pods home. Bob Erickson who grew up in rural Wilmar, Minnesota, told me their one-room school, grades one through eight, would close for a day or two to let the students gather milkweed pods. I then asked Pastor Harry Hillman of St. Cloud. He lived in Michigan during the war, and the kids there picked milkweed pods too. That was the same answer I got from Jay Gunderson of Foley, Minnesota, who lived in Wisconsin as a child in the 1940s.

Milkweed grows wild in the country. Farmers aren't happy when it grows in their fields. It has a heavy root system, and it's hard to rid the field of the pesky plants. The stalk stands about two feet high, and the seed pod is about the size of an egg or a fist. Within the pod is a cotton-like white fiber. When the drying pods begin to crack and the fiber starts to show, that is when they are ready to picked.

I asked why the military was so eager to acquire milkweed pods. I got two different answers. Some had been told as children that the fiber was used in parachutes; some said the cotton-like fiber was to be used in life vests. It was buoyant and good for flotation devices.

Shortly after the country schools started in the fall, the milkweed pods were ripe for picking. The plants grew wild in the ditches, woods, along the railroad tracks and fence lines. They secreted a milk-like substance, and the kids would get sticky and wipe their hands on their clothes. Climbing in and out of the ditches wasn't easy, and dirt stuck to their sticky hands and clothing. Mothers had to love that.

They carried mesh onion sacks to hold the pods as they worked. The filled sacks were hung up back at the school or home while the pods dried. If they weren't dry, they could mold and not be useable. Trucks came by the schools to pick up the dried pods or were taken to collection points.

I wondered why, if the milkweed was so vital, the government didn't just grow it in fields like any other crop. There is a reason. It takes three years to grow sturdy milkweed plants, which makes fields unusable for food crops the army also needed. And time was crucial. But the pods were already available, mature and free for the picking in the rural areas. All that was needed was pickers to harvest the crop. Children were ready harvesters. They were inspired to do the sticky, dirty work and understood it would save the lives, especially of the Navy men and paratroopers.

Keeping track of a whole school of kids as they picked their way through the countryside had to be a monumental task. Besides the mesh onion bags, they had to bring their lunches along. The older kids handled that and the ditches well, but the little ones struggled.

Mothers had to deal with the results of the pod picking excursions. They had to wash the sticky, dirty clothes as well as doctor the scrapes and bruises of the young children. Since girls always wore dresses, their bare legs had to get scratched. It was a united effort to save the lives of military men.

I never heard of milkweed pod picking. I was raised in the city. But since I began working on this book, I've heard a chorus of voices of the seventy- and eighty-year-olds who told in detail of their milkweed pod picking expeditions during World War II. They were proud then, and they are proud now for the work they did to help in the effort to win the war.

I really felt I missed something as a child when I learned that country children did such a big deed and I didn't know about it. I was determined to experience picking milkweed pods. In fall of 2008, I drove into the country to start my hunt for milkweed plants. Immediately I spotted a patch of milkweed standing on the far side of the ditch. I grabbed my camera and a bag to put the cut pods into.

The ditch was deeper than I thought, and there were rocks. I was afraid of twisting my ankle. Once across the ditch, I took several pictures, then picked some and put them in the bag. I had enough of milkweed pod picking really fast.

A car came down the narrow dirt road. When the car stopped, I noticed the occupants were a middle-aged man and woman. He rolled his window down and we conversed. I explained about the milkweed pods I was carrying, mentioned the book I was writing and that I wanted some first-hand experience about the milkweed pods. He told me he knew all about the milkweed pods used as flotation devices during the war. The cotton-like fiber was packed in waterproof material and made into life vests.

Shortly after that, I ran into a man in a local grocery who shared stories of being a child during the Depression and World War II. His family ate depression stew to ward off hunger pains. He said his mom got a kettle of garden tomatoes in the summer and used canned tomatoes in the winter months. She would slice the tomatoes, add water and cook them until they were hot, then add homemade noodles. That was it. They ate it day after day. He survived the Depression on that stew. We ate oatmeal and pancakes. We survived too.

I asked him about milkweek pods. He said out in Avon, Minnesota, where he grew up, they picked their fair share of pods. He didn't know what they did with them, but he knew it had something to do with the war. "It was a good thing to do" was what he was told. He said he was never asked to pick millweed pods for any subsequent war. I told them what they were used for, and he liked that idea and hoped he had helped a sailor.

U.S. SENATOR DAVE DURRENBERGER'S EXPERIENCES

I was a first grader at St. John the Baptist School on the St. John's campus (also known then as PS 120 of the Cold Spring School District) when World War II began. I well remember our fall forays for milkweed pods, filling our gunny sacks (into which we also picked potatoes from the abby farm at the appropriate time. Other recollections include eating St. John's bread with lard instead of butter. The same order of German Benedictine nuns, who baked the bread and fed the abby, university, and the prep school, taught us. Dairy products went straight to the war effort, so, much to my parents' chagrin, I drank coffee at an early age.

Other recollections include gas stamps that limited auto travel, air raid alerts when we had to pull down our curtains at night, getting our news by radio or the RKO Pathe newsreels at the Paramount, Grand or Eastman theaters in St. Cloud or the Cold Spring theater where I saw Judy Garland as Dorothy in *The Wizard of Oz* for twelve cents. I also kept scrapbooks, one being an old wallpaper catalog into which I pasted newspaper and magazine clippings on the war. I have vivid memories of the U.S. Army Air Force cadets who did their basic training at St. John's for two years under my athletic director father. Jack Webb, the TV actor who played "Joe Friday" on *Dragnet* was one of them. There was a wall on the main quad at St. John's with the names of Johnnie in the military service and gold stars with those who died—all of whom I remembered because the college was so small or my dad knew them well.

11

Knitting for the Servicemen

Yvonne remembers vividly how her Mother, Ruth Eckman, would bring home a basketful of skeins of khaki-colored yarn from the Red Cross office during the war years. She knit man-sized sweaters and caps until she ran out of yarn. The finished clothing would be taken back to the Red Cross office, and then Ruth would load a basket with navy-blue yarn and repeat the process knitting for the Navy. Then it was back to the khaki yarn again, then another basket of blue. She was doing what she could do to help with the war effort. She used her time and talent to made clothing to keep soldiers warm. This wasn't a leisurely activity, like knitting when she was in the mood. She knit far into the night and was at it again first thing in the morning. No one kept count of just how many she made.

How many women like Ruth knitted warm military clothing items until their fingers ached and their vision blurred? They were true Americans motivated by love and concern. Freely they shared their talents to make things better for the fighting men.

Bill Morgan lived in Pipestone during the war. He recalled being in the third grade in the public school. The first hour of the school day was devoted to activities to help the military. The students could choose between knitting four-by-five-inch squares, which women would later stitch together for afghans for the soldiers recovering in military hospitals. The second choice was sawing round checkers from broom handles using hand saws. The checkers too, were sent to the wounded in hospitals. Bill said he pictured recovering soldiers under the afghans the grade school children made playing checkers. This work wasn't a choice but a daily assignment to aid the injured as they recovered.

One rainy evening, I met my brother-in-law Jay Gunderson and his wife, Louise Baker Gunderson. It didn't take long for the conversation to get around to World War II. Jay told me he picked milkweed pods in Wisconsin for the military. His one-room country school took a couple of days off each early fall to go out and gather onion bags full of milkweed pods that the military used for making flotation devices.

Louise talked about attending Garfield Elementary on St. Cloud's southside. She, too, said they knit afghan squares. This wasn't done on school time though; she took yarn home and knit in the evening. The school supplied everything, the yarn and the needles. Money was tight at home, and there would have been no way she could afford this project. Louise recalls that the yarn was wool because there were no synthetic yarns at that time. The school only gave out small balls of yarn, of all colors. It was probably all donated from school families. She was never given a fresh skein of new yarn. The knitting needles she used were natural too, either bone or glass.

Louise liked to knit, and she could do it well. She felt good about doing something for the soldiers in the hospitals. When she turned in her work, she was praised.

When the milkweed pods were ready, Louise said her class was taken to the edge of St. Cloud were they picked the pods. This was the only city school I know of that harvested the pods.

12

Tragedies at Home
Shortages and Ingenuity

T he dreaded polio found its way into our house. My youngest brother, Dale, age two, was stricken with infantile paralysis, which left him with a limp arm and sagging shoulder. When he walked, he struggled to keep his balance. There were public warnings posted on how to prevent the spread of polio. We were told to avoid contact with other people as much as possible. In particular we couldn't invite friends for sleepovers, nor could we sleep at our friends' homes.

Dale lost his balance and fell often, so dad dug out the blue stroller from storage. I can still picture him with his one arm hanging limp. He used his good arm to fight off anyone who tried to put him in the stroller. Dale didn't like to be confined like a baby again; he'd tasted freedom and this was hard for him.

When Grandma Elizabeth Genz came to the house, she said, "We have to pray. The baby is sick. This is serious." So we prayed.

Mom took Dale on the city bus to the doctor's office to be checked regularly after the polio was diagnosed. The doctor put Dale on the waiting list for the Sister Elizabeth Kenny Institute in the Twin

Cities. Sister Kenny was an Austrialian nurse known for her work with polio victims. We didn't have a phone, so mom would go to the neighbor's to call to see if the doctor had any good word from the institute. The plan was that mom and Dale would take the Greyhound bus to the Cities when the call came. Dad and Grandma would take care of us. Mom would stay with Dale.

We waited. Grandma's plan took hold. Dale began to have movement in his arm, and eventually the arm was completely restored. We were a thankful family and knew enough to thank God for this miracle. The stroller was put back in storage.

We again focused in on the war activity.

TRAGEDY IN ANOTHER HOUSEHOLD IN THE WAR YEARS

Albert Schulte was desperate to keep his family fed. He lived with his wife, Olive Young Schulte, and their four grade-school children: Bert, Mel, Tom, and Patty. Their home was at Twelfth Avenue South and Eleventh Street South, St. Cloud.

When Albert learned the government was hiring civilians to work on a secret mission out of the country, he applied. Those were desperate times, and the family had huge needs. The job paid well. He was sent to Gander, Newfoundland, Canada, to work along with other civilians and the military to build an airplane landing strip needed by the armed services. Necessity called Albert out of his homeland. He was trying to take care of his own.

Albert was in Newfoundland when tragedy struck at home. His six-year-old son, Tom, just returned home from first grade at St. Mary's Catholic school. The Kurr Ice company truck was parked in the alley behind the neighbors. Tom climbed on the truck to get a piece of ice. When the driver started to move the truck, Tom fell under it, and it ran over his leg.

The leg was broken, and there was talk of amputation. Olive had the government official reach her husband in Newfoundland, and he was on the next military cargo plane back to the states. The leg was saved after a steel plate with six screws was implanted. Tom's recovery was slow. Albert never returned to Newfoundland.

The job had already provided money for new jeans for school for all the kids. Tom cried when the medical people cut away his new jeans to free his broken leg. The new jeans his dad worked to provide for him were wrecked. New jeans were hard to come by.

Wartime activities that seemed to dim when tragedy hit home began to come back into focus as the child healed.

CHILDREN EXPERIENCE SHORTAGES

As a young child, I was aware of shortages of a number of things the family experienced during the war years. None were life-threatenting, but of some concern. Food and gasoline were skimpy sometimes. I know how carefully my mother handled her nylon stockings because they were always in short supply. The military had need of the nylon for parachute ropes. Collection barrels set out in stores where women could donate hosiery with runs. Occasionally the local downtown stores would get a few nylons. Word got out that nylons were available, and the ladies would practically run across the bridge to get to the stores before the supply was gone. Some would take the city bus hoping to get to the stores first.

Patty Weihrauch Cruser, of Sartell, told me of the ordeal her mother, Sarah, and she went through to get a pair of nylons for Patty to wear to the all-important occasion of Confirmation. She was in eighth grade. At the last minute, they learned that Fandel's Department Store in downtown St. Cloud had nylons in. They were seconds, less than perfect, but they were the coveted nylons. Together, Patty and her mom stood in a long line waiting they turn at the counter, fearing the store would run out before their turn came. The supply lasted, and they were able to go home with their seconds for Confirmation.

Sheets were scarce too. I was just a kid and wasn't interested in nylons or sheets. The army also needed what the rubber plants produced to make supplies for the military. That shortage cut back on making a favorite thing children loved, bubble gum. To substitute for real bubble gum, companies made a chewable substance from wax. Some of it came in the form of a whistle. We could blow the whistle, and when we were done playing with it, we could chew the wax like gum. It was flavored but, we couldn't blow bubbles with it. Some people I interviewed said they chewed on tar newly laid on the street.

Rita Bechtold Reker, of St. Joseph, Minnesota, just west of St. Cloud recalled bubble gum being scarce in her town too.

Our house was across the street from Wilson Avenue Grocery in the 300 block of Wilson Avenue Southeast. I remember one day I got word that bubble gum had arrived at the store. I got my nickel and ran to the store to get five pieces. "Wally-over-at-the-store," as we called the store's owner, so as not to mix him up with anther Wally we knew, would only sell me two. He said he had to have enough for all the kids in the neighborhood, and he couldn't give me five pieces. He knew how many kids frequented his store and he wanted to please them all.

The government didn't ration the bubble gum, it was Wally-over-at-the store who put limits on it. He knew us all by name, and it wouldn't pay to go back later and try to buy another two pieces. Even if I changed my clothes, he would still know me.

Another shortage due to the restricted rubber was elastic. Mothers made underwear for the girls, and elastic was essential. Moms had to substitute something. Buttons would have to do. Yvonne, who I mentioned earlier, told me how the button came off her underwear when she was swinging on the monkey bars on the playground at Roosevelt School. The underwear fell to the ground. She jumped down and picked it up, put it under her arm and ran all the way home. She vowed never to go back to school again unless the underwear had two buttons.

Some mothers didn't know how to sew or how to make button holes. Their daughters wore drawstring underwear. It was difficult for the little girls to keep their underwear tied. Sometimes they got knots in the strings and cried in the bathroom until a teacher came to help them. These are not major things, but we had to learn to cope.

Sibyl, my great helper in writing this book, shared what she experienced as a child with leg paint. When women couldn't buy nylons, they resorted to buying leg paint, which they applied to their legs. It gave the appearance of looking like nylons. With an eyebrow pencil the ladies could then draw a line up the back of their legs so it would look like the seam nylons had. How they managed that, we don't know.

The leg treatment lasted more than a day and didn't wash off. It had to wear off. Sibyl told how her mother, Clara, met a friend in a Five and Dime store. While the ladies were visiting, Sibyl noticed the lady's legs were more than one color.

She got down on her knees for a closer look and saw the legs were peeling like a sunburn. Later it was explained to Sibyl that the lady didn't have any nylons, so she painted her legs to look like nylon stockings.

WARTIME COINS

The high demand for copper for shell casings and other things during the war brought about the temporary discontinuation of copper pennies. The pennies that replaced the copper ones were made of steel and covered with zinc. They were called "steelies" or "white lead" pennies. I saved them in a mustard jar.

Dale and I were playing with our penny collection, both the copper and the steel. Dad told Dale to get a magnet from the junk drawer and to see which of the pennies would stick to it. The wartime money stuck, but the copper pennies did not.

With the end of the war came the return of the copper money.

INGENUITY PREVAILS

There were so many limits put on the American people that it took some creativity on their part to get around them.

Women told me they dealt with the shortage of sugar by keeping bees. Honey was a good substitute for sugar. If they didn't have bees of their own, women made arrangements to buy honey from bee keepers.

Ralph Stangler of Sauk Rapids lived with his family on a farm in St. Rosa, Minnesota, during the war years. At one time, the family car needed four tires. His dad didn't have enough money or rationing stamps to meet that need. One day when he was driving past a farm store, he spotted a used farm trailer with four yellow wheels with decent-looking tires for sale. The price was right, and he didn't need rationing stamps for used tires. The trailer wheels fit on the car, so there wasn't any need to change them. How much better deal could he get! So, he put the yellow wheels on his green car and a huge problem was solved . . . all done legally and cheaply!

One woman told me her parents struggled to make the allotted coffee last until more stamps would be honored. They learned from some neighbors with the same problem that drying dandelion roots and crushing them could be used as a coffee substitute. Dandelions weren't seen as blight anymore. They had a fourteen-year-old son who liked coffee but was too young for coffee-rationing stamps. He wasn't old enough for the draft either. Stretching out the coffee by adding dandelion root seemed to solve the problem until the war came to an end and more coffee was available.

Theresa Steichen Thiesen told me her brother serving under General Patton somewhere in Europe sent a letter home to his mother asking her to send him a bottle of whiskey. Under ordinary circumstances, she might not have answered the request, but those were not ordinary times. She bought the bottle of whiskey, took it home and had an ingenious plan about how to get it to her son in tact. She shaped a clump of yeast bread dough a little longer than the bottle of liquor and baked it. When it was done, she hollowed out the loaf, put the whiskey bottle inside and tucked as much of the remaining bread around the bottle as she could. Next the opening was covered with the cut-off heal of the bread. She boxed it and sent it to Europe. When word came back that the son received the package in good shape, the family was happy. It gave her son a break from his grueling times.

Darlene Daniels Dols lived with her parents, Ben and Agnes Daniels, and four siblings near our family home in northeast St. Cloud. The grandparents of these children lived in Anoka, about fifty miles away. They were lonesome for the grandchildren but couldn't break away from all their farm work to drive to St. Cloud to visit with the family. Ben was short of gas rationing stamps and couldn't make the round trip to Anoka. His dad, being a farmer, an essential worker, he was allowed extra gas. He coaxed Ben to come to Anoka. He said, "If you have enough gas to get here, I can give you enough to get back home."

Darlene remembers the trip. She said it took forever. There was a wartime speed limit of thirty-five miles per hour meant to save on gas and tires. If caught speeding, the judge could order the speeder to lose his gas rationing stamps as well as pay a fine. At that speed, the fifty miles to Anoka took a very long time.

Ben Daniels wanted to go a step further than the Victory gardens. He decided to raise chickens to supplement the rationed meat. He put a chicken coop on his city lot by his garage and bought chickens. In spite of his best efforts, raising chickens didn't go well for him, and he abandoned the project. The end result was that the kids had a chicken coop for themselves. They made it into a library, store and assorted other ventures. Dad's failed attempt at raising chickens provided for the kids something to occupy themselves during the summer time.

CLARA PHILIPSEK NEIS
WHERE THERE'S A WILL, THERE'S A WAY

Clara Philipsek Neis lived with her parents, Tom and Frances Philipsek, and several brothers and sisters on a farm in Stearns County, west of St.

Cloud. Clara completed eight grade in one-room country school Number 10 near her home. To continue school, she needed to go to Central Junior High School in downtown St. Cloud. Grades seven through nine were in this building. There were no buses to transport students from her area for the eight-mile trip to school. Fortunately for her, her dad, in addition to farming, had a job in St. Cloud, so he could provide the daily round trip.

Central Junior High was one of the stops Mrs. Eleanor Roosevelt made on her whirlwind visit to area schools. It was a privilege for Clara to see her. It was a major event in her life, and she remembers it well.

The bombing of Pearl Harbor was just ahead. Gas and tire rationing was to follow shortly. Clara wanted to attend a second year of high school, but it looked bleak since her dad no longer worked in St. Cloud. She connected with a family living near Technical High School. At only fourteen years of age, she worked for them for room and board. She could continue her education and was determined to do that, in spite of the war. The war never broke her young spirit. Where there is a will there is a way.

This was not the case at the Philipsek farm house because they had many younger children. I was told that other farm families with sons at war in foreign lands and their daughters rooming in town to get a high school education, found it too quiet in the farmhouse. No school bus service and gas tightly rationed closed the options of going to high school unless the girls could room in town. The parents now had much more time to dwell on their sons in battle. World War II drastically rearranged families.

MARY BRUCE AUSTIN

I was eating lunch in the dining area at Whitney Senior Center in St. Cloud, Minnesota, when a woman rolled up to my table in a wheelchair with her lunch tray and joined me. I was glad for the company. We exchanged reasons why we were at Whitney. I was there for a class on

"How to Get Your Book Published," and she came every Tuesday and Wednesday to play Whist.

Mary told me she was in the wheelchair because of World War II. She had to work so hard at a young age that it took its toll on her. She lived in Villard, Minnesota, as a young teen and had to lift 100-pound feed sacks when she worked around the farm. So many men in the area had answered the call to go to war that there weren't enough left to do the farm work. There weren't men to hire at harvest time. Some women stepped in to do the labor to keep the farm running. Handling the feed sacks at thirteen was only one of the things Mary had done. She is paying the price in her older years for the hard labor of her youth.

I asked her if she ever picked milkweed pods for the military, and she said, "No, but my brother and I tried smoking them. Dad rolled his own cigarettes, so we had the paper. We crushed up the milkweed pods and smoked them."

In a sense, Mary—like so many other women of the times—is a casualty of war. Necessity caused her to work beyond what a young girl could handle physically. In the toll of the war, Mary and women like her need to be in on the count.

Five-year-old Gerry Winter (third from left) poses in the Red Cross nurse's outfit her mother, Elizabeth, hand sewed for her. Three of her neighborhood friends stand with her, dressed in their military uniforms. Left to right: Ron Pearson, unknown, Gerry Winter, and George Salters. Gerry's two oldest brothers were in the military. Gerry Winter Thielman lives now in Sartell, Minnesota, and has lived in Minnesota for forty-one years.

13

Children in Military Clothing

Dressing the children in military clothing, often to match the branch of service where an adult member of the family served, seemed to be a choice a number of Americans made. When a Navy father would return home, he could be met by his little toddler son dressed in a navy outfit too. It was cute.

Mail order houses sold children's military clothing, both boy's and girl's, to match all division and some ranks of the military service. The cost was from three to seven dollars complete with hats, helmets, dress jackets, belts, and gloves.

My mother sewed many khaki-colored army jackets complete with brass buttons for little boys. Of course, Dale had one of them, so did his boy cousins, thanks to mom.

George and Bertie Sears's oldest son, Sam Sears, was a pilot in the army. His parents bought a complete army outfit for their younger son, George. They were so proud of both of their "military" sons.

My friend, Gerry Thielman, now of Sartell, had a Red Cross nurse's uniform hand sewn by her mother, Elizabeth Winters.

The young boy in the sailor outfit is Ronald Ruhoff who lived in St. Cloud. He is the son of Rudy and Marcella Ruhoff. His mother sewed this detailed military uniform for him.

George Sears wanted to be the image of his older brother, Sam, in the service.

The Winter family lived in Wilmette, Illinois, at the time. Gerry had two older brothers in military service. She remembers their pictures posted in the window of the Woolworth store in downtown Wilmette. She was proud to see them whenever they were in the area. She told me Blazer's Barbershop in town had about fifty pictures of military men and women pinned up. We surmised customers brought in the photos. Gerry doesn't know why her brothers were in the window at Woolworths. The brothers both came home decorated soldiers.

When we were children, we would see boys in grade school or at the park wearing military clothing. We would walk circles about them looking at every detail. It was big stuff to have one of those outfits, some complete with badges and medals.

I don't know of any wartime since then where children have dressed so much like miniature military people, though there still are "navy" outfits for girls on store racks, and a great array of clothing has been made out of camouflage fabric, but it generally doesn't mimic adult uniforms, and girls' "middies" were around for girls long before navy clothing looked like them.

MORE HOME FRONT EXPERIENCES FOR YOUNG CHILDREN

Other youngsters experienced affects of the war too. Mary Ann Czek Skelton was born when her brother Bernard was away from home in active duty in the military. Their parents were Joseph Czek and Elizabeth Skudlarek Czek. There were several other children in the family as well.

Their family home was at the edge of Holdingford, Minnesota. Mary Ann remembers being three years old and playing outside. Her mother was nearby milking a cow. Mary Ann cried out to her mother, "Mama! Mama! There's a stranger on our road!" Mother got up from the milking stool to look. It was her son Bernard coming home from service. He put down his duffle bag and picked up his sister who he had never seen. It was their first meeting.

There wasn't a phone in the farm house for Bernard to call for a ride. I heard this repeated several times. Valiant soldiers often came home unexpectedly. Because communication was so poor and many rural homes had no phones, they had to walk from the bus or train depot to their homes. Some hitch-hiked and got dropped off reasonably close to home. They often ended up walking the last miles home from the war.

Ray Fitch, son of Roy and Rose Fitch, now lives in Sartell, Minnesota. He was just a baby when his only brother Erwin went into the military. Erwin had a chance to see his baby brother before he left.

Erwin's tour of duty took him to North Africa and Italy. He was gone nearly five years. As the years passed, Ray grew too. When Rose wrote to Erwin she would have Ray write and drawn on the margins of her letters. The advancement of the drawings made Erwin realize how long he

had been away from home. The war took so much time away from building family relationships, lost time he hoped to make up.

WAR-TIME CHRISTMASES

In the United States we celebrated four Christmases with family members away involved in battles in other countries. What was it like to gather for Christmas when dad was spending Christmas on another continent in the throes of war?

Children of a widowed mother remember their four Christmases during the war years as being very somber. A flag hung in their window with one, two, then three stars on it. They had three brothers in harm's way. It was difficult for their mother to make the house seem festive. She brought out the box ornaments but only

Raymond Fitch, Minneapolis, had been told he had a brother, Erwin, in the military. He had no memory of Erwin, but he had a uniform like his brother's. Ray lives in Sartell, Minnesota.

put up a few. Each of the younger children received one gift. The expectation and wonder of Christmas was gone The church service remained the same, but home was too quiet. Mother always kept one eye on the driveway for the military car and men to be arriving with bad news from the War Department.

Then came Christmas of 1945. The war was over. Two sons came home quickly, and the third one would be home soon. It was an exceptional Christmas! The war was over! No need to watch the driveway anymore.

Some children of the World War II era can remember very bleak Christmases. Unfortunately war still overshadows Christmases for a great many children.

14

The Red Cross

Not all that I saw in the newsreels was the horror of war. Sometimes I saw people from the Red Cross organization in action, doing what they do, helping people. Even as a child, I picked up on the respect felt for the Red Cross for the tremendous help they were to others.

There was a Junior Red Cross group for children in school. We had arm bands with Red Crosses on them and tin Red Cross pins to wear on our shirts. I kept that Red Cross pin in my jewelry box for decades. I remember learning how to bandage.

One of my friends across Wilson Avenue from me marched in a hometown parade. She was one of four girls who carried the Red Cross flag. The flag was white with a large red cross in the center of it, similar to the one displayed on the front of the table shown in the picture. Each girl held a corner of the flag, carrying it open and flat. As they walked along the parade route, spectators tossed money onto the flag as the girls walked by, making a donation to the Red Cross.

Recently I was visiting with this friend, and she reminded me of a gold-star mother (one whose son had died in the war) on our side of town. This woman was always so sad looking because she lost her son in the war. It was remarkable that, as a child, she had been able to identify sadness in the older mother. The war affected the children, making them more aware of some kinds of things.

Eight unidentified children put money in a Red Cross collection box. (Courtesy of the Stearns History Museum - Myron Hall Photo Collection)

15

Mother Becomes a "Rosie the Riveter"

Dad went to work for Char Gale, a newly formed defense plant in St. Cloud on Thirty-third Avenue North. The company moved into existing buildings that formerly were used to manufacture the Pan motor cars. Dad called it the "war plant." The escalating war needed a flow of new airplanes. This local plant made steel airplane wings and fuselages. Dad was thankful for the full-time work that produced equipment the military direly needed to win the war. The steady income made home life better for all of us.

A multitude of young people left our hometown to go into battle for our country. So many that one block of homes had the window military service banners showing twenty-one in service from that block alone. It was Fifteenth Avenue North between First and Second streets. They called it "Blue Star Avenue." Before going into service some of these people had been employed locally, and their jobs needed to be filled. Char Gale hired as many men as were available, but had so many openings they started to recruit women to step into those vacant positions to keep production going.

This neighborhood in St. Cloud (Fifteenth Avenue North between First and Second streets) had twenty-one residents in service simultaneously. Stars in the windows reflect this. (Courtesy the Stearns History Museum - Myron Hall Photo Collection)

Some kids at school talked about their mothers going to work to help build airplanes. I couldn't imagine this. Up until this time, I had known of only one mother in the neighborhood who was employed outside the home. I always pictured mothers wearing housedresses and aprons and staying close to home and their children. I was totally unprepared when mom made the announcement she was going to learn how to rivet and planned to go to work at Char Gale. She took a class at the local high school and passed the riveting class. She told us she was a good riveter. Mom was on her way to becoming "Rosie the Riveter" as the wartime song went.

The required dress code for women at the plant was slacks, a blouse, and also a turban to cover their hair. Mother never liked nor wore slacks, but she made that concession. I went with her to get some "yard goods" as we called fabric, so she could sew slacks for herself. I can clearly remember her sitting at her treadle sewing machine with Dale on her lap when she was making the new work pants. I watched her peddle that machine for a long time, turning out a pair of slacks and a turban. I didn't like this at all. Mom didn't seem like mom any more. She was so busy.

She had to work the night shift and left in the dark. She rarely went anywhere without Dad in the daytime. Now she was going to be out alone at night in the dark and cold. She had to catch the bus to get

One lady riveting and one inspecting at the war plant. (Courtesy of the Stearns History Museum - Myron Hall Photo Collection)

to the war plant to rivet on airplane wings. Bus transportation was a must for the employees. So few had cars and the rationed gas added to the dilemma of getting to work.

I had on my pajamas and watched her make her sandwich of homemade bread and put it in a bag for her lunch. She didn't look like mom in slacks. I just didn't feel safe like I used to.

In the morning Dolores made a big kettle of oatmeal for all of us. Mom got home as she promised, in time to braid my hair for school. Dale went to a sitter so mom could sleep in the daytime.

Sometimes when we got home from school, Mom would have a copper boiler of water on the kitchen stove heating to be put in the washing machine. She did laundry for the eight of us after supper in the wringer washer in the kitchen. Two tubs of rinse water sat beside the machine. The wet clothes were kept in baskets overnight and mom hung them on the line in the morning when she got home from work. In the winter, she hung the clothes on ropes strung up in the kitchen.

Mom's working as Rosie the Riveter seemed to take a bite out of my life. The tempo at home had changed. Contentment was gone.

On the plus side, I knew our soldiers were getting good equipment because my mom was helping build it. Then there was mom's first payday. On Saturday, both Nita and Verna got brand-new never-worn-before shoes! They got to pick what they liked! We all got a turn at that in the weeks ahead. Dad wouldn't have to be repairing our shoes too often anymore. That was exciting.

Alvina Fleck, a long-time friend, told me she too worked at Char Gale as a riveter. Just teenage girls, she and some friends drove in from the family home in the country. With gas rationing, they could only get four gallons a week, so coming any distance was a problem. Alvina moved to St. Cloud and shared an apartment with a girlfriend. She talked of taking the bus to work. Cars were still scarce. On payday, many of the workers from the war plant treated themselves to chow mein at the O.K. Restaurant in downtown St. Cloud.

Mom didn't work very long; it was just too hard on her, and I was glad. But she had had a taste of being out of the home and missed paydays.

My cousins, LaVon Eberhardt and Joyce Kreger, quit Tech High school and took a bus to California to work in the shipyards. Joyce's father,

Ray, was already working out there, and the girls stayed with him. They put sheet-metal duct work into ships. The war moved families into new dimensions of living. The sons were off to war at a young age and the girls were given permission to work. Their parents Cecil and Loretta Eberhardt and Ray and Lyall Kreger would never had allowed this action of the girls in peace time.

This mobile float served as an advertisement for Char Gale of St. Cloud, where parts were made for World War II airplanes. (Courtesy of the Stearns History Museum - Myron Hall Photo Collection)

16

Victory
The End of World War II

I n the April of 1945 we had both of our Victory Gardens plowed. Before we got it all planted, Dad heard Hans von Kaltenborn announce on the radio that President Roosevelt had died. We were in shock. What now? Vice-President Harry Truman was sworn into office. The war continued. Before the month was up, the news of another death filled the airways. Hitler had died! The war was winding down now.

I remember that summer day in 1945. Late in the afternoon, we heard that the war was over. We didn't hear it on the radio. We heard the church bells ring from the other side of the Mississippi, which was odd at that time of day. Cars drove by honking their horns, and people began shouting, "The war is over! We won! We won the war!" Dad wasn't home from work yet.

People started streaming out of their houses, banging kettle covers together and shouting, "The war is over! It's ended! We won! We won!" Mom dug in the cupboards to find kettles and spoons for us to pound. We ran out in the yard making our share of noise to celebrate this historic event. I couldn't believe it when I saw Mom come out of the house with our birthday cake dishpan, and she was hitting it with a wooden spoon. We had been so careful not to chip the dishpan, but all caution was thrown to the wind. Today Mom was beating on the birthday cake dishpan. Neighbors came out and hugged and cried in the streets. Sons and daughters would be coming home! What excitement! What relief!

A guy on the southside of town shot his gun (and shot down the telephone wire by accident), we learned later. Later there were many organized celebrations, but this spontaneous one in our front yard is the one I remember the best.

We gathered around the radio when Dad got home and heard the news from Washington. It was official! World War II was over!

Some unwinding from the war had to take place. There were some post war activities. Dad wondered if we could go back to where we were before the war. Could we transition back, or had we changed too much? Could we ever be interested in just our own little town again? The war permanently enlarged our world.

War posters came down. The Schools-at-War flag was put away. There was no need to buy war stamps. No one needed us to donate used iron. Ration books weren't needed. Service men still crowded at the Greyhound bus depot, but now they were on their way home. No more children had to fill onion sacks with milkweed pods. No need to sit out blackouts at home or hide under the basement tables at school. Enemy planes would not be overhead. Hitler wouldn't scare me anymore. But star flags hung in the windows a long time following the war. People were not anxious to put them away. They were so proud of having sons serve in the military. The flags were like badges of honor.

My stomach didn't hurt anymore to hear Hans von Kaltenborn on the radio. He said good stuff now. What a relief! I hoped we would never have another war. I could finish my grade school years in peace!

In just a few weeks Dale had his fifth birthday. Mom said she only hit the birthday cake dishpan on the outside, and it was fine. We put five candles on the dishpan birthday cake. It was a perfect cake and a perfect day. Life would be better for us all.

17

Two Families with
Five-Star Flags

HELEN KARDASH LANDOWSKI'S FAMILY

Helen Kardash Landowski lived her childhood years in rural Sauk Rapids, Minnesota. She was the youngest of thirteen children born to John and Lucy Kardash. Her father farmed and was also employed in Sartell.

Helen's sister Marcella was a registered nurse and decided to join the army. Next her four brothers Thomas, John, James, and Robert went into the military in various branches of service. One by one they left the house to go to boot camp.

The atmosphere of the home changed with five family members serving in the armed forces and in harm's way everyday. The family was on the receiving end of much prayer, as were all the families involved in the war from Sacred Heart Parish in Sauk Rapids. Whenever Lucy stopped by the church, people would pray for her, knowing she lived with much tension and slept very little. These prayers meant a great deal to her and helped lift the burden she carried.

The war ended eventually, and all the Kardash children all came home. Not one had been injured! One son contracted malaria, but that was the extent of health related problems. For the time they spent battle in foreign lands that was truly amazing.

Each homecoming sparked a new celebration. Mother insisted, however, that each of them leave their duffle bag outside the door. She wanted the bags emptied out on the lawn and sorted through just to make sure they would not be bringing foreign critters of any kind into the house.

During the time they were gone, the military service flag with five blue stars hung in the window of the porch so all who came around would know five young adults from the family were in the armed services. The family was so proud of them and took pride in displaying the window flag and all it represented. They were ever so thankful none of the stars had to be changed from blue to gold, denoting that someone from that household had been killed in the war.

Helen is my neighbor in rural Sherburne County now. I was impressed when she told me she had five siblings in the military during World War II. She was the first one with whom I had spoken who had had a total of five family members in service simultaneously. She shared further that all four of her brothers have since died. Her sister Marcella married a military man and made their home in Chicago and never made Minnesota her home again. They had fifteen children. Marcella was ninety-six at the time of this writing.

FRED REKER'S FAMILY

Fred Reker of St. Cloud spoke of his childhood that took place during the World War II years. He was the youngest son of Fred, Sr., and Catherine Reker. There were nine children in the family living on the family farm in Lismore, Minnesota, in the southwest corner of the state.

He recalled that his church, St. Anthony's, in his hometown, had twin bell towers that were lit every night. They could be seen for miles

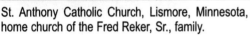

St. Anthony Catholic Church, Lismore, Minnesota, home church of the Fred Reker, Sr., family.   Fred and Rita Bechtold Reker.

around the farming country. After the bombing of Pear Harbor, American cities practiced blackouts, periodically turning out all street, business and residential lights. The purpose of this drill was to make towns invisible if the enemy planes were flying in the area. The darkened towns could not be spotted, thus escaping destruction. The church remained dark for the remainder of the war years. The darkened towers loomed over Lismore, seemingly matching the darkness people felt during war time. The familiar lights were out.

The third oldest of the seven Reker sons was Alvin, who was serving with the National Guard. He was on a ship headed for the Philippines when Pearl Harbor was struck. He was far from home, and the family knew he was in danger. This family had never traveled far from home, except across the boarders into Iowa and South Dakota to visit relatives. Many prayers were said for Alvin, who was on the other side of the world!

One by one five of the Reker sons went for their army physicals. Only Roman did not pass due to an old leg injury. Edwin, Milo, Sylvester, and Raymond were in various branches of military service. With war declared Fred, Sr., had five sons in active duty fighting for their country. Roman remained at home along with the two sisters, Irene and Viola, and Fred who was thirteen. There was always the concern that United States could be bombed.

Fred, Sr., with his huge investment in the war, monitored the war as closely as he could by listening to the radio broadcasts as often as he could. They had a Coronado radio in the house with aerial mounted outside to catch the signal, so they could hear news from the other side of the world.

The prayers were many at the St. Anthony Catholic church for the war, especially for the sons and daughters of their own parish. It wasn't just the Reker family who had multiple sons gone to war. The absence of the young adults was felt in the farming community. This became especially evident at harvest time. There just weren't extra farm hands available to hire to help. Working with a skeleton crew was about impossible. Some of the business men in town went out in the evenings to help with the harvest. Even the town cop, who was the only law enforcement person as well as the street maintainance man, managed to help harvest every summer. There was only one stop sign in town, so traffic violations were minimal. People couldn't deny helping the fathers of Lismore who had sons and daughters in the armed forces if it was at all possible. In the front window of the Reker home was a flag displaying five blue stars. Under ordinary circumstances these five willing and hard-working sons would be home lightening the load at harvest time.

Christmas was another time when the absence of so many children was felt. Christmas at the Reker household included attending midnight mass together and going to church again in the morning. A big dinner followed. The five sons were missed.

One thing Fred mentioned about rationing was they had meat rationing stamps they didn't need because there was meat for them on the farm. They used the stamps to buy the more processed meats, like lunch meat, that was a treat.

On the Coronado radio Fred, Sr., learned of the sudden death of President Franklin Delano Roosevelt. Fred, Jr., said his dad typically didn't show much emotion but came near to crying at this news. He was not of the same political party as the president, but he believed the president led the war well. It was a hard job and FDR had done his best.

One by one, the same way they left, Fred's five brothers came home. The family was so thankful the flag in their window had only blue stars. The Lord answered the prayers of this family to bring all its sons home to Lismore.

Fred was now old enough for college. His teen years had been filled with the tension of the war, but now that was over. He was about to get on a train and leave Lismore to go to college in New York, where they had more than one stop sign. The church bell tower lights came on again. All was well.

Andy Virden, Waite Park, Minnesota.

As a child, Andy remembered playing on a Civil War cannon in the school yard at McKinley Elementary. When he was a teen, the cannon was donated in a scrap drive and pulled out of town. Herman "Gooner" Bartz asked around for a picture of the cannon. Former Mayor Al Ringsmuth recalled the cannon but wasn't aware of pictures. Eddy Bauer found a picture among those of a deceased Waite Park native. Walt Pederson, St. Cloud native and member of the Plaistad Snowmobile Expedition to the North Pole, also remembered a cannon near a high school in his hometown of Duluth. That cannon was also donated for the World War II effort.

18

Three Families Pay the Ultimate Price for Freedom

W hat were you doing when you heard President Kennedy was shot?" This question was common following the death of President John F. Kennedy. This was such a shocking event, most people remember clearly what they were doing and how they heard of it. The devastation of 9/11, the collapse of the twin towers, was another event marked by most Americans with exact details of what they were doing when they heard this news.

So it was with the bombing of Pearl Harbor on December 7, 1941. Those who experienced that event remember the details of when and how they heard the news and what they were doing at the time.

THE VIRDEN FAMILY

Andy Virden, a native of Waite Park and a retired St. Cloud businessman, has excellent recall of his initial hearing of the bombing of Pearl Harbor. He was just thirteen years old at the time. He was outside in the backyard with his brother Al, who was working on the family car. His older brother, Joe, was in the house listening to a football game. The broadcast was interrupted by the announcement that the Japanese had bombed Pearl Harbor. Joe ran outside and shouted to his brothers, "Pearl Harber has been bombed. Americans were killed."

The whole family—Andy's parents, Andrew Daniel Virdena and Clara Imdieke Virden, as well as his three brothers, Al, Joe, and Ralph—gathered to talked about the bombing. They were stunned. Andy can't believe, even now, that the family went ahead with planned afternoon activities. His mother had promised to take Andy and his friend Herman Thomas to a movie in St. Cloud. The guys didn't get the car running, so Clara and the boys took the bus to the downtown movie theatre. A few minutes into the movie, the camera was turned off and the house lights came on. The theater manager announced that the Americans had been bombed at Pearl Harbor. Again there was shock and disbelief, but the movie then continued as planned.

The next morning at St. Cloud's Central Junior High School were Andy was in the eighth grade, his Social Studies teacher, Mr. Paul Bixby, brought a radio into the classroom. President Franklin Delano Roosevelt was going to address the nation regarding the attack on Pearl Harbor. Andy and his classmates heard the speech, which began, "Yesterday, December 7, 1941—a date that will live in infamy—" There was such heaviness at school, home, and all around town.

Just a few weeks prior to the president's speech, his wife, Eleanor Roosevelt, had made a brief but historic visit to St. Cloud, and she took the time to visit many area schools, including Central Junior High. At that time Andy was losing his sight from an eye condition, but he was still able to see that she was dressed all in black. It was great to see the first lady of the land. Now this! How could it be?

When older brother Al graduated from St. Cloud Technical High School in 1942, he enlisted in the Army Air Corp. He had a short furlough after his basic training. Andy particularly remembers that Al could buy gasoline for the car without needing a ration stamp. It was a perk for military personnel home on leave. When Al had to report back for duty, Andy rode along with the family to bring Al to the St. Cloud Greyhound bus depot in downtown St. Cloud. It was to be the last time he saw him.

On July 21, 1944, Andy's dad came home early on the hot afternoon. He said, "There's something wrong." Andy remembers his dad pacing around the yard and repeating this many times. The elder Virden didn't know what was wrong, but something definitely was. It was so very hot that afternoon. Still troubled, Andrew went back to work out on the farm. This memory is fresh in Andy's mind even after sixty plus years.

A few days later, Andy, sixteen at the time, was home alone in the family's Waite Park home. He answered a knock on the door. There stood a man from the Western Union telegraph office holding a telegram from the War Department for his parents. They were both working. Andy told the man his mother was working at the St. Cloud Laundry in downtown St. Cloud. The Western Union man got back on his bike and went to find Clara at her job.

The message was the Al was missing in action. Andy couldn't remember if his mother took the bus or a cab home, but he could remember how hard she cried. His father was called, and, before long, he was home, and the family gathered. They recalled Andrew's premonition just days before when he kept repeating there was something wrong. It was true; something had been very, very wrong.

The military informed them that Al was declared missing in action. He would be declared dead in one year if he didn't turn up in a military hospital or on a list of prisoners of war. His body could also be found. And there was always that chance he was still alive.

Andy recalls the horror of that year. There was a cycle of emotions: agony, despair, and hope that a mistake had been made and Al would turn up somewhere. These emotions went round and round as they waited for further word from the military. It was very hard on the family and was a horrible year for them.

Andy was at Tech High School by then. There was no formal counseling there at the time. But his teachers were very supportive, and Vice-principal F.J. Herda was too. Andy's brother Al had just graduated two years earlier, and the faculty remembered him well. Other students at Tech had suffered family losses as well. The staff showed how much they cared in many ways. Vice-principal F.J. Herda and Principal Elizabeth Clark attended memorial services for the students whose families were suffering the loss of someone close. Andy expressed an appreciation for that support.

At the end of the year, the military declared Al dead. A flag and an array of military medals were sent to the Virdens. The family wanted a grave marker in the Waite Park cemetery even if they had no remains. They bought a plot and had a granite tombstone erected with his name, military rank, birth date. The marker stated that Al had died in World War II. Young Andy stood in the huddle with the family around that site.

In spite of all this, Andy wanted to be in the military, but his blindness made that impossible. He said it was extremely hard on him as a teen to know his parents were in such deep grief over the loss of their son. Andy grieved for them. World War II and the resulting death of his brother overshadowed his teenyears. He wasn't old enough to be in service, but he was old enough to know the pain of war. Pain lessened with time, but Andy Virden was a Minnesota child who took a hard hit on the home front during World War II.

Word did come to the Virden family from returning prisoners of war in 1945 with details the family needed to know. Al had died on June 21, 1944, the day his father came home saying something was wrong. Al's plane was shot down over Germany and all but two of those on board parachuted out and were captured. Al and another man went down with the plane and were killed. The military put a bronze marker on the grave. This marker included some details not known at the time Al was declared dead.

Clara Virden became a Gold Star mother. A flag with one gold star hung in the window.

I called Fort Snelling National Cemetery in Minneapolis to check if they, too, had sites marked for those missing in action and with no remains. They were quick to answer, "Absolutely." That seemed so right.

SHARON EBERHARDT SCHULTE

THE HOFFMANN FAMILY

I have known Larry and Marie Winkler Hoffmann of St. Cloud for decades. Larry told me about his older brother Wilfred, nicknamed Bruno. Bruno was determined to join the United States Marines at an early age. He was anxiously waiting for his eighteenth birthday when he would be eligible to enlist. He graduated from Cathedral High School in St. Cloud in 1941 and was working at the *St. Cloud Times* as an apprentice stereo typesetter. He had started working for this local paper as a carrier boy and moved on to the mail room and now to typesetting.

Even before he was eighteen, Bruno got his Mother, Olivia Hoffmann, to sign for him so he could legally join the marines. Shortly after boot camp was completed he was sent to the South Pacific theatre of operations.

The *St. Cloud Times* office, where Bruno had worked, had a banner hung where it could be seen easily by the public. A star was placed on this banner representing each employee that left the paper to be in military service. They added a blue star to the banner to represent Bruno.

Larry, fifteen at the time, was alone in the living room of the family home on St. Cloud's south side, on July 31, 1944. It was already a day charged with emotion. His father, William Hoffmann, was in the

Marie Winkler Hoffmann and Larry Hoffmann.

hospital struggling with throat cancer, and it was his mother's thirty-ninth birthday. A man riding a bicycle clearly marked "Western Union" rode up the sidewalk to the Hoffmann home. When the doorbell rang, Larry opened the door to a guy with a telegram in his hands from the War Department. It was for either Mr. or Mrs. Hoffmann. Larry got his mom, and she immediately knew it was bad news. Bruno had been killed in action. Larry said, "She took it so hard." This family now knew the real horror of war. His dad had to be told in spite of the fact that he was very sick and weak. Death came to this family when they were already experiencing great stress. Bruno had been killed on the island of Saipan. His body could not be returned to the United States immediately. The logistics of getting supplies to the fighting men superceded the need to get bodies of the deceased back home. Bruno was buried along with other American military men on foreign soil.

Five months later, William Hoffmann, the father of the family, died in December of that year, 1944. Larry lived out his formative teen-age years in the shadow of all this.

Bruno's star on the banner at the *Times* was changed from blue to gold. Bruno was the second of the former *Times* employees to be killed in action. Bruno's mother was a widow and a gold star mother.

At the request of the family, Bruno's remains were brought back to the United States in 1948, four years after Bruno was killed, and a service was held at the Cathedral of Immaculate Conception Church in St. Cloud. Bruno was reburied in Calvary Cemetery just a few miles away.

The casket flag was presented to Olivia Hoffmann the day of the reburial. Time has put this flag into the hands of the next generation. It is in Larry's home now and highly treasured.

When Larry was an adult he was in the Korean Conflict. He told me when he was in Korea he was shot out of a jeep on the Fourth of July. Odd that it was July, the same month, years earlier, in another war in a foreign land, that his brother, Bruno, had been killed in battle.

MARIE WINKLER HOFFMANN

Marie Winkler Hoffmann, wife of Larry Hoffmann of St. Cloud, shared with me that her brother, Donald Winkler, who was in the Minnesota National Guard, had been sent to Greenland with his unit during World War II. Their mission was to build a landing strip for a refueling stop for war planes.

In a short time, the family was notified that Donald was missing from the construction site in Greenland. It was cause for great concern. The family was promised more information in the days following. No information came. It was hard for the family as days turned into weeks and they still heard nothing. Marie was eight years old

The Winkler family was members of Holy Angels Church on St. Cloud's north side. They owned Winkler's Grocery, a neighborhood grocery store, also on the north side.

A family prayer meeing was called, and the Winklers closed the store for this. The parish priest came to lead the prayer meeting at their home as they didn't want to leave the house, thinking word about Donald could come anytime.

They were on their knees in prayer when Donald walked into the house. Marie said it was so, "uncanny." They were shocked! Donald didn't know he had been reported missing. Communication was poor during World War II.

The prayer meeting turned into a praise meeting. This was one war story with a good ending!

THE SCHMITT FAMILY

Dennis Schmitt had his own war story. "I was six. My four oldest brothers were in the war. We lived just outside of St. Joseph. It was summer time, and dad went out the back door after supper to work in the garden. I went out the front door followed by Mother and my three younger sisters. We played in the front yard, and I was a ways away from them. We weren't out there very long before a car I didn't recognize came down our road. The driver drove up close to where Mother was standing. I stood real still. I knew this was something important. Serious. Two soldiers wearing uniforms got out of the car. It was a coupe. Maroon. I can remember exactly where it was parked.

"It was like everything stood still. The men went over to Mother and one of them gave her a piece of paper. I later learned it was a telegram from the War Department. Mother put her apron to her eyes. The men's mission was complete, and they got back into the car and drove away. She went to the backyard and talked to Dad.

"I can picture all of that just as plain as day. I know exactly were everyone was standing. Everything seemed to stand still. I just stood there and watched it all. I was six."

Denny's parents got the four younger kids and the older kids who were home together and told them their oldest brother, Alvin, had been in killed in the war. The telegram read, "We regret to inform you . . ."

The family learned that Alvin, twenty-six, had been killed in New Guinea. Tears and grief came to all of them. Probably the little ones didn't understand and cried because everyone else was crying.

Dennis "Denny" Schmitt.

I asked Dennis if he remembered going to the funeral, thinking he would tell about a flag-draped casket. Instead he told me there wasn't any funeral. Apparently there was so much action that boats and planes were needed to bring supplies to the fighting men. They couldn't get the bodies back to the United States. Alvin had been buried in Manila. A memorial service was held in the Catholic church in St. Joseph.

When the war was over, his parents were contacted and asked if they wanted Alvin's remains returned to America. They did. They didn't want him to have a permanent grave in a foreign country. Alvin was reburied in Fort Snelling National Cemetery in Minneapolis. Dennis said he remembered some of the family going down to Minneapolis, but for some reason he didn't go.

He didn't know how much time had elapsed from the time Alvin died until the body was shipped back to the United States. I emailed Fort Snelling. They said the remains came back in 1949, five years after he was killed. Dennis was eleven at the time of reburial. As an adult Dennis went to Alvin's gravesite.

I was able to fill in some missing facts for this family and made a memory book about Alvin for them. All the other brothers came home from World War II, and a flag with stars hung in the window of the Schmitt home. The family's flag had one gold star and three blue stars.

Alvin's casket flag was given to his parents. In time Dennis inherited the forty-eight-star casket flag and is proud to have it. Dennis became a World War II buff and knows where all the battles were fought. Still, he remembers when the maroon coupe came to his house and he learned of his brother's death when Dennis was six.

When Dennis was an adult he chose to go into the service and served twenty-six months in the Panama Canal Zone.

How many American children heard the news firsthand, along with their family about the family member was killed in World War II? They were on the scene when the soldiers came to their house in the military car, or they answered the door when the Western Union man rang the door bell.

It was traumatic for some of them to see their family consumed in shock and grief. Some told me they never saw their dads cry before. Families had much to cope with, and some children didn't speak the questions troubling them. The war wounded the kids on the front lines at home. No one gave the battlefield yell, "Medic! Medic! There is a child wounded over here! Help!"

I thought it interesting that each of these men had his brother's casket flag, passed down in the family. Each was proud to inherit it and keep it in triangle-shaped display cases. Family ties ran strong and deep through the generations. Soon these precious flags will be passed on to the third generation.

I wanted to help these families I interviewed. I wanted to fill in some missing facts for them. I hunted up newspaper articles when they asked for them. Together we visited the Veterans Bureau so they could get military records. Fort Snelling staff answered questions and supplied us with pictures of tombstones so those family members who had never been to the cemetery could see the inscribed marker. It felt good to help these families even if it was sixty-five years after the fact.

One daughter said her dad never told her about his experiences as a child during the war. She was happy he told me. Then she could write about it in the family history book. The children of World War II have stories to tell that are well worth preserving.

Both Denny and Larry said they chose to go into military service when they became young adults.

I well remember the young men riding around St. Cloud on bikes that had Western Union signs attached to them. The men wore caps also inscribed with 'Western Union."

We never at anytime had a telegram delivered to our house for any reason, and I don't recall anyone we personally knew getting a telegram. How awful that job had to have been, to deliver a telegram to a home from the War Department. Surely they knew the message contained in the envelope they carried and had to dread delivering it. They heard the first, "Oh, God! No!" They couldn't get away fast enough, down the steps and onto their bikes on the sidewalk to avoid hearing the screams and agony taking place in the house behind them. Western Union men would have some stories to tell as well. Young American children lived behind those doors the Western Union men visited and saw chaos take over the family. Family life was never be the same after that.

19

Rooted Memories

EVELYN BOROS OOTHOUDT - LITTLE FALLS

I lived everyday of the war," Evelyn Boros Oothoudt said of her memories of World War II. She lived in Little Falls as a child with her parents, Alois and Angeline Boros, and five siblings. An older brother was in the service along with five uncles and some cousins. That was a great number of relatives to have serving in the military simultaneously. They corresponded regularly by Victory mail (V-mail), which was a light- weight sheet of writing paper that folded into its own envelope. It could be a month or two before they received a reply from the men in foreign countries. The letters from the fighting men were censored so as not to give away details of location in case they fell into the hands of the enemy. Mail time was much anticipated at the Boros household.

Evelyn Boros Oothoudt.

Alois would bring a pickup truck home from his place of employment, and the truck would have some things on it that had to be taken to the city dump. In the evening, the family was anxious to ride along to the dump, hoping to search for copper. The word was out that there was a shortage of copper. The military needed it to manufacture radios. They hunted in the dump for anything copper, even old radios with copper wire were a good find. The family knew where the copper collection center was in Little Falls. They turned in what they found as fast as they could so that new radios could be made for the service men. It was a rewarding family adventure, and they did it as often as they could.

The children attended public schools in Little Falls. When the schools did things to promote the war effort they participated. Instead of recess, students combed vacant fields for milkweed pods to make parachutes. In ninth grade a student brought in a small swatch of something white and silky—a piece of a parachute.

At St. Francis Xavier church, the Boros family was grateful for the opportunity to take part in everything the church did for the military men and their families. There were many times of prayer and services for the American fighting men. Two former alter boys from the church, brothers John and Bob, joined the service. Evelyn can remember the last time she saw John walking along the railroad track with a dog and carrying a stick. His brother was a pilot in the navy. Both of the Little Falls brothers were killed in active duty. Evelyn's brother Claude, accompanied John's body home for burial. Evelyn was the younger sister, and she observed this. A flag with two gold stars hung in the window of the boys' family home. She saw it hundreds of times. It was a reminder of the horror of war. She attended the funeral of the older son at St. Francis Xavier church. At a young age, Evelyn was acquainted with the hurt of war.

The Boros family, like most American families, dealt with shortages of food, shoes, soap, gasoline, and coffee. They tightened their belts. Little Falls had community blackouts, and the neighborhood grocer was a block warden. They practiced making their town dark so it wouldn't be visible to the enemy to attack from the air.

On Decoration Day, now known as Memorial Day, parades held a special excitement with so many military men involved, local bands, and all the flags being carried. Evelyn was a Girl Scout during the war years and the Scouts had a big role in the parade. The girls walked in formation, carrying large bouquets of purple and white lilacs. Some had spirea flowers. The parade route took them across the Mississippi River bridge. When the Girl Scouts were on the bridge, the parade halted, giving the girls time to go to the bridge railing and toss their flowers into the water, commemorating the deaths of service men at sea. It was a moving thing for the young girls as well as the spectators to watch. At the end of the parade route, the girls climbed into army trucks and were taken to the cemetery where they placed more flowers on the graves of veterans. They learned at a young age to honor the dead.

People gathered in St. Cloud on the St. Germain Street bridge for a Decoration Day ceremony. Flowers were tossed into the Mississippi River to commemorate the deaths of service men at sea. Girl Scouts generally were the ones tossing the flowers. A bugler is on hand to play taps. (Courtesy of the Stearns History Museum - Myron Hall Photo Collections)

The Boros home was near the north end of Little Falls, near the railroad tracks. The family knew all the train whistles, and, during the war years, Angeline, Evelyn's mother, could easily identify the sound of a troop train passing through. She said it was different. She would call out, "Troop train. Troop train," and whoever of the family was at home would run outside and wave to the soldiers as they passed by. The neighbors would respond similarly, and the soldiers on the train would wave back.

Their neighborhood had several vacant lots near the tracks. The military used these empty places to set up temporary army camps. Army tents were erected and military men moved in. Here they waited for their next orders either sending them overseas or on to their respective camps.

Sometimes the troop train would stop, men would disembark and other men might board the train. Army trucks would come around too and could have this same exchange of men.

The town's people interacted with the soldiers at this temporary holding camp. Adults in town engaged in conversation with the young soldiers far from home with a heavy mission ahead. Certainly some of the locals had sons of their own off serving the country and offered encouraging words to these special men.

The soldiers often walked over to watch the Little Falls children roller skate on the cement of the tennis court and played with them. One Spanish-speaking soldier from Texas had a guitar. He played and sang and taught the Boros children and others how to sing three songs in Spanish. The children loved it. He said one of the little girls reminded him of his five-year-old daughter in Texas. The family became attached to this soldier and corresponded with him for a time after he moved on. The Boros family wondered what happened to him and the many others they had had the opportunity to know personally while they stayed in the tent camp.

Finally, the center stakes of the tents were pulled, and they came down, and the temporary camp was gone. The Boroses felt a loss. Evelyn treasures this childhood memory of the camp in her neighborhood.

Hearing this information about tent camps prompted me to do extensive research. But no newspapers from that era had photos or stories of the camps. Even people at Camp Ripley, just north of Little Falls, didn't know much about this, and they were around during World War II. I believe that, with the emphasis overseas, what happened behind the scenes at home didn't rate the news.

Bernie Reimer Waldorf, the sister-in-law of my friend Marge Waldorf Skelton, lived near the tents as a child and now lives in Grey Eagle. She said her family rented rooms to a Colonel Cook and his wife, and Cook might have been in charge of the camps. Cook sent a Christmas card to her mother for years until she died at the age of ninety-three. Bernie also remembers taking homemade buttered bread to some of the tent dwellers.

Evelyn recalls going to movies about the war, starring such greats as John Wayne and Van Johnson. The scripts were written to make these men heros. She said it seemed like Van Johnson could win the war all by himself. She found the movies to really boost her morale. The neighborhood children would re-enact these movies in their backyards. Many battles were fought and re-fought in the children's playtime.

Through the newsreels, Evelyn became acquainted with President Franklin Roosevelt, Churchill, Stalin, and, later, Tojo. When they got the word that President Franklin D. Roosevelt had died, deep sorrow filled the family. They mourned.

Shortly after that came a time of great rejoicing in the United States when the citizens heard that the war was over. It was over! Done! What relief! A burden lifted! The sons and daughters of Americans would be coming home! Halleluia!

The war wasn't "over there" for the Boros family. For them the war was "up close and personal." This family was so loyal, they did all they could in their family, church, school, and community.

It was by accident Evelyn and I connected one day at the Whitney Senior Center in St. Cloud after many years of not seeing one another. She shared her story with me. I didn't quite know what she meant when she said, "I lived every day of the war." Now I do.

BILL MORGAN - PIPESTONE AND ST. CLOUD

For years after World War II, Bill writes, Aunt Anne Winters joked about how she ruined her dustpan by donating its rubber strip to one of the war's rubber drives. As a survivor of the Great Depression, my aunt never would have wasted fifty-cents on a new dust pan from the Ben Franklin store in Pipestone, Minnesota.

From 1942 to 1945, Americans participated in blackouts, plane-spotting, and scrapdrives—activities supposed to help everyone feel as if they were playing a vital role in the war effort. To some extent these endeavors also kept us from worrying about our relatives overseas.

A blackout was a nighttime exercise that required people to turn off their lights and draw their shades. Had an enemy plane flown over southwestern Minnesota, the pilot supposedly would have had a hard time finding Pipestone or, more importantly, the airbase in Sioux Falls, sixty miles away. Older citizens were designated block-wardens and given military ranks. Mother was a lieutenant, and Aunt Anne a sergeant. Their assignment entailed walking around our neighborhood during blackouts looking for people who had neglected to turn off their lights.

Mother and I were also trained to spot enemy planes. Had a Zero, Stuka, or Messerschmitt flown over our town, Mother's job was to alert the base in Sioux Falls. (I'm not sure we truly believed that the Germans or the Japanese might actually bomb our corner of the state.)

For years, Mother and I emptied tin cans, cut out and placed the tops and bottoms inside the cans, and squashed them underfoot until they were pancake-flat. Once a month, the manager of the Orpheum Theatre invited kids to bring their can-filled grocery sacks downtown where they were weighed in front of the theatre. The boy or girl with the heaviest bag earned a free movie ticket that otherwise cost twenty-five cents.

Scrapdrives were often showcased by a Main Street parade. During one scrapdrive, the town's treasured Civil War cannon—the showpiece of our courthouse square—was ignominiously dragged backward down Main Street, headed for some distant scrapheap.

Children wait in line to donate newspapers for the war effort. (Photo courtesy the Stearns History Museum - Myron Hall Photo Collection)

That day, Mother decided to discard an ancient sewing machine pedestal and thought it would be fun for me to push or drag it down Main Street. For a costume, Mother found a tall, thin cardboard box from which she cut holes for my head and arms. On all four sides of the box, she wrote in large letters, "STITCH UP THE NAZIS." Its tine metal wheels proved so cumbersome that I had to abandon the machine in front of Dibble's Garage, three blocks from home. Still dressed in my cardboard suit, I marched down Main Street while puzzled spectators wondered what my now meaningless message meant.

Tires, sugar, meat and gasoline were rationed during the war. Rumors spread about certain people who hoarded these goods or sold them on the black market. When our local butcher offered Mother a cut of sirloin steak—an item few people legally ate in those days—she refused to take it because, she said, "I have three boys in the service."

I was eleven years old on D-Day. Months after that event, we learned that brother Alan had gone ashore on Omaha Beach. After landing in Normandy, he walked across Europe with the First Division. Later, during the invasion of Germany, Brother Loran, a battalion surgeon, parachuted into Germany where he survived the jump though landing in a tree. My brother Stan, who was almost too old to join the service, enlisted in the Navy, though he stayed stateside.

When the war ended, these three men—my heroes—came home to a country where foreign powers no longer threatened our freedom.

DICK AND ROSE SNOW MARTINSON - ROSEAU AND DETROIT LAKES, MINNESOTA

I had the pleasure of visiting with Dick and Rose Snow Martinson of St. Cloud. They spent the World War II years as children living in northern Minnesota. Rose is the daughter of Charles and Emily Snow, and they lived in rural Roseau, Minnesota, seven miles from the Canadian border. Rose has two sisters, Fern and Lillie, and two brothers, Chester and Robert.

Rose mentioned the military had need of cattails. She said she went out and picked cattails and put them in burlap bags. Rose understood the cattails would be used to make life jackets and other flotation devices for the servicemen. There was a collection point where they were turned in, and the military men picked up the gunny sacks of cattails.

Saving bacon drippings in a tin can on the back of the stove seemed to be a popular practice for many families. Rose mentioned this and seemed unsure just what her family did with the full cans. I remember a sign in a local butcher shop that said, "WE BUY USED FAT." The housewives received four cents a pound for it. Numerous reports I found suggested the fat was used in making glycerin, and that was used to ignite explosives. The military needed used fat.

Dick Martinson spent his childhood in rural Detroit Lakes, Minnesota. Besides his parents, Alfred and Maureen, Dick had two brothers, John and Alfred, Jr. Dick said the nearby town of Lake Park, Minnesota, had a Community Cannery run by a Mrs. Reno Bergeson. People could bring produce from their victory gardens, and their meat, to the cannery to be preserved. It was convenient, safe, and much hot water was available. It was sanitary. The food was not put into glass jars but into tin cans, eight cents for a small can and ten cents for a large can. This apparently had to be a huge help to families in the area to have their own Victory garden food processed under pressure in the Community Cannery.

Dick told of having a Red Rider BB gun during his boyhood years. When the fighting servicemen had a high demand for copper, the copper covered lead BBs were no longer available on the market. They were replaced by just plain lead BBs and they were not as powerful, nor as effective as the former copper-covered ones. The kids understood these actions; it was important to them, and they still remember these sacrifices.

Rose said, "I can vividly remember when the war ended. I was standing on the kitchen stoop when that news came over the radio. I was elated. I knew then my future brother-in-law would be coming home."

Rose Snow and Dick Martinson married and moved to St. Cloud a number of years ago.

GREG PAPPENFUS - ST. PAUL AND ST.CLOUD, MINNESOTA

Dr. Greg Pappenfus, D.D.S., of St. Cloud, had the opportunity as a young boy to experience a rather astounding war-related event.

His grandparents, Charles and Alice Alstatt, lived on a bluff in St. Paul. Directly below the bluff was the Homan Air Field. Young Greg looked forward to the times his parents, Clarence and Barbara Pappenfus, would take trips to St. Paul to visit his grandparents. Sometimes he would connect with his cousins, Paul and Jerry Hunt, there. The three boys would sit in Grandpa's backyard and look at the Homan Field down below. They watched as trucks brought in assembled sections of airplanes—wings, tail pieces, and some fuselages. Bomber planes were being assembled in the buildings below.

Greg had been to Char Gale, the St. Cloud-based defense plant, with his dad and watched trucks being loaded with completed wings and other plane components. In St. Paul, he watched as some of these same plane parts were being unloaded from flatbed trailers.

The boys' attention peaked when a hangar door opened and a brand new, shiny bomber was rolled out onto the field. The plane was about to go on a test run to get the bugs out. Greg clearly recalled the planes had four engines. They would fly directly over his grandfather's house. The three young observers would get a really close look at the underside of the plane as it came up over the bluff. The roar of the four engines would make them catch their breaths, and their hearts raced.

Greg remembered crawling onto the roof of the carriage house and waiting for the bombers. He marvels still at the beauty and excitement of it all. After a brief flight, the plane landed and taxied back to the hangar. Greg said he would never forget the roar of the planes.

This is a powerful memory of World War II. Greg observed at close range the equipment that would be sent into battle. The planes left Homan Field to go to another location for the installation of their machine guns and other artillery to make them war ready. They would then be sent to battlefields on the other side of the world.

Blackouts

Clarence Pappenfus, Greg's dad, served as a blackout warden in the neighborhood of their home in north St. Cloud. His uniform consisted of a white helmet with an insignia and a belted jacket. He carried a special flashlight with a beam that would not give away his location.

When the sirens blew, Clarence was on duty. Blackout drills were treated very seriously. Greg said he and his friends' imaginations would run wild. They believed the Germans and Japanese would bomb them.

Saving Gas for the Trip to the Cabin

Greg's dad saved gas in one-gallon glass jugs in the garage. He'd use his rationing stamps to buy gas and put one of these gallons into the glass jug. The family had a cabin in the Brainerd area, and it took ten gallons of gas to make the round trip. They counted the cans many times to see how close they were to getting a trip to the lake. As often as he could, Clarence would add one more gallon to the garage jugs.

Good Buddies

Neighbor kids banned together during the war. Greg mentioned a good friend, Allen Heuerman, who lived next door, and another buddy, David Shereyak. They were part of the war effort and spent time crushing cans and adding to the scrap drives. They knew about rationing stamps. Signs of war were everywhere. When they were walking, they noticed the blue and gold stars in people's windows. The sight of a Western Union guy on a bike always got their attention, especially since someone near the Pappenfuses had a War Department telegram delivered to their house.

Celebration

A good memory Greg holds is the family celebration when Uncle Wilfred Pappernfus came home on leave. He looked great in his uniform, and the whole family was so proud. Uncle Willie again went off to war and came home a second time. He worked as an electrical engineer.

Grandpa Provides Furs for the Military

When Grandpa Alstatt got word that the military needed fur to make soldiers' clothes warmer, he responded in a big way. He was an outdoors man, enjoyed fishing, hunting and trapping. Greg was interested in Grandpa's new endeavor! Grandpa said fur from the wolverine was best. Beaver and muskrat fur shed water and was good for parka hoods. Fur collars were put on the cold-weather flight jackets. Grandpa started trapping. Once the skins were dried, he turned them in. Three generations of this family were strongly connected to the work of being at war.

JEAN MOBERG - DULUTH

Jean Moberg knew exactly how she first learned of the bombing of Pearl Harbor. She was in the car with her parents on a snowy Sunday afternoon in Duluth. They were on the way home from a matinee. The car radio was turned on, and the news reported the Japanese attack on the Americans at Pearl Harbor. Her parents realized that war was ahead for the country. Her mother was thankful for the fact that Buddy, their son, was only thirteen years old (though the war lasted long enough for Buddy to join the Navy when he was seventeen years old).

Jean attended Lester Park Elementary School in East Duluth. She bought war stamps and collected aluminum for the scrap drives. Jean was taught to knit in school, so she could help make afghan squares. Ladies stitched the squares together making coverings for the soldiers in military hospitals. There was much for the children to do at Lester Park School.

The family lived near the railroad tracks. They took advantage of an offer made by two railroad companies in Duluth. The railroads allowed the residents to use the property adjacent to the tracks. This railroad right-of-way could be used free of charge to plant Victory gardens because of the

These twelve neighborhood Duluth children are dressed to be part of a parade on London Road celebrating the end of World War II. Jean Norrish Moberg, who sent in the photo, called it the "First Armistice Day Parade." It was held on August 17, 1945. Most of the dress portrays the military. The picture was published in a local Duluth newspaper. Left to right: Carol Rude, Virginia Glibbery, Mary Jo Agnew, Beth Agnew, Curtis Anderholm (in the wagon), Jim Hagen, Barbara Suech, Jean Norrish, Roderick Rude, Frederick Glibbery, Charles Beaupre, and Tom Hagen.

high demand for food the troops needed. Jean said this was a free lease for the nearby residents to plant their victory gardens.

Jean's father took a block-long site from Fifty-sixth to Fifty-seventh Street East. He planted a variety of vegetables during these years for the family's use. It was a family project. Jean remembers some people used their free garden plot to cultivate raspberry bushes. Jean said that today raspberries still grow in that area, probably remnants of the original plantings.

Jean recalled her father saving some of his gas rationing stamps for her brother, Buddy, to use when he came home on leave. He wanted him to be able to drive around Duluth when he came home.

Jean wanted to share a favorite family story that came about during the war years. Buddy, although out of the country, was aware of the chewing gum shortage at home. He mailed Jean a case of chewing gum, twenty-four packs. Her friends became very excited about the windfall of gum that came their friend's way. They asked Jean if she would make out a will listing them as beneficiaries of the gum in case something happened to her. Gum was a hard-to-come-by treat. The family needed a little humor. She has retold this story many times. It was funny then and is funny now.

Jean well remembers the first Armistice Day parade. She and her friends were in a local parade on London Road celebrating the end of the war. They were all dressed up for this occasion and their picture was taken.

DAVE BORGESON - DULUTH

Dave Borgeson was eight years old and attending Lakeside Grammar School in Duluth when Pearl Harbor was bombed. Life changed drastically for the Borgeson family at home, in school, and in the community.

Two of Dave's older brothers, Roger and Donald, were in the National Guard. Their unit was called up immediately, and they were off to war. Two more older brothers, Art and Glen, joined the navy. Dave's dad was a World War I veteran. When civilians were being hired to work on a military landing strip in Greenland, he decided to take that war-related job. He was glad to be doing something for the war effort and also earning money for his family in Minnesota.

Dave's mom, Idena, was solely in charge of the six children and the task of keeping the house up and running. The children had to work in the garden in the summer and shovel snow in the winter, among many other chores, work that had been done by those who had left for the war.

There were three sisters in the home, Marjorie, Joan, and Betty. Dave was referred to as the "man of the house" at age eight. He had twin brothers, Tom and Bob, who were seven years old.

The seven sons in the family had shared an attic bedroom with three double beds and one single. With four brothers in the service, each of the younger brothers had his own double bed.

Dave said the word WAR was seen and heard everywhere. At school, a work project was devised for the children. The janitor made small square weaving looms by pounding a row of nails on the four outer edges of a block of wood. The school staff considered it hazardous for young children to use knitting needles, so these looms were considered safer for them. The students were to weave squares that the ladies later would stitch together into afghans. When completed, the squares would be taken to the Red Cross office in Duluth to be distributed to wounded soldiers recovering in hospitals both in this country and abroad.

The children also helped make slippers for soldiers. They cut out from fabric, using a pattern, what he described as footprints. A top band was needed, too, to snug the slippers to the feet. The students of Lakeside Grammar School were only instructed to cut out the slippers, so that ladies could sew them. Dave tried sewing a slipper once, but it didn't go very well, and his mother had to fix it. After that, Dave stuck to the task of cutting the pieces out.

Citizens of Duluth were encouraged to donate whatever materials they could to local scrap drives. Idena, with the children's help, cleaned out the garage and home of any items they could spare for the scrap drives. They found metal, rubber, glass, tin, and old papers, which they put in separate piles on the lot next door. The junkman wouldn't pick up the offerings unless they were separated. It was a huge undertaking for Idena and the children.

War was on all the newsreels at the local theaters. Newsreels made war easier to understand than the papers.

Dave said Duluth was considered a prime target because the iron ore that came into Duluth from the iron range was shipped to steel mills. The military needed the steel for military equipment. There was a constant movement of trains and ships carrying ore. If Duluth were bombed, the United States armed forces could be crippled. Dave used to lie in bed at night listening to the sounds from the harbor. He knew when he heard the ships and the lift bridge "talking" that all was safe, no bombs had hit the harbor.

Dave talked of the extreme measures students were taught at Lakeside Grammar School to get to their homes safely in the event of an air attack on Duluth. When the air raid warning rang at their school in the late afternoon, they didn't hide in the basement as other students did. Instead, they were to connect with their assigned neighborhood group and run for home. They were not to run on the street or sidewalks, though, but to use the alleys, go between garages, so they could not be seen by the enemy in an air bombing of the city. They could cross streets and sidewalks but not run parallel to them. They watched for bombers all the way.

Dave was a Police Boy at school, stopping traffic at the crosswalks for the students. He was chosen a Junior Air Warden for the air raid drills. He had to guide a number of children from his neighborhood and practice ways to get home as quickly and safely as possible. When they came to a child's home, the group stayed nearby, undercover, until that child was safely inside, and then moved on to the next child's home. Three in Dave's group lived beyond him, and he had to escort them home first before he could run back to his own house. The next day a report had to be given to the teacher on how well their plan worked. The children were to evaluate the course they had taken and make changes that would allow them to run home faster the next day.

The children in the Borgeson family also had to gather coal that fell from the coal cars passing through. They used this coal to heat houses in the winter. Adults working in the area gathered much of the coal, but the young boys had trouble with this. Counting the cars in the train was more interesting than picking up lumps of coal. When they got to their home or Dave's grandma's home the reward was the same—they got cleaned up, were given hugs and cookies no matter if they picked up a lot of coal or not.

Mail delivery was a major event every day at the Borgeson house. It was their sole contact with the five men who were gone. Idena worte to the the family members as often as she could. Replies were slow in coming, though, due to troup movements. The mailman was held in high regard. Dave was grateful for the letter writing skills he learned in school. He was taught the right format for a letter. Dave wrote the first copy of a letter, and then made four more copies, so his four brothers and dad would each receive one. He was taught the right way to address envelopes, too, so that his letters weren't always put in with his mother's letters. He could write independently of his mother.

After the letters were sent, he waited along with his mother for the mailman to come to the house. Military personnel on all fronts greatly looked forward to mail call and getting letters from home. On the other side of that, families at home anxiously waited for word from a son, husband, father, brother, daughter, sister because word meant they were alive, at least when they received the letter from home. The coming of the mailman was so anticipated that women often called others on their block to let them know the mailman was on the way. If there was one person that everyone knew where he was a most times, it was this person. Dave said that when his mom got word that the mailman was near, she would send him running out to get the latest letter into the box before the mailman arrived. Idena had so many to write to with four sons and a husband gone from home plus a son-in-law and a nephew, that she spent a lot of time writing. Still, it could be a month or more sometimes before she would get a reply to her letters. As time passed without word, anxiety rose, only to be relieved when a letter came.

Three times young Dave learned of war deaths. His oldest sister, Marjorie's husband was killed in Normandy. One of his school friends's father died in battle. A cousin's family received one of the dreaded telegrams from the War Department informing the family of the death of their son.

The new widow, Marjorie, had two young children. She went to work, and Dave babysat his niece and nephew.

Idena was awarded an emblem of honor because she had four sons in the service. She wasn't much for public displays, but she did attend the induction and had her picture taken with eleven other mothers from the Duluth area who were honored for having four or more sons in service. Her picture was taken for the *Duluth News-Tribune* and was published November 5, 1943.

When the war ended, Dave's dad and all his brothers came back home. The attic bedroom again had seven brothers sleeping together, just like the old days. But it was really never the same. The older brothers missed so many years of being part of the lives of the rest of family, they soon moved out and began lives of their own.

MARCIA BUCK SCHUT - MINNEAPOLIS
THE WAY WE PLAYED DURING WORLD WAR II

During World War II Marcia Buck Schut lived in south Minneapolis with her parents, M.E. and Rachael Buck, and her younger sister, Janice Buck. Her dad was generally called, "Buck."

In their home, patriotism was high and from the womb. They were raised red, while, and blue. They learned to pledge their allegiance to the flag with their hands extended. They were very aware that there was a full-blown war going on. In play, everything became a rifle, machine gun, or a bayonet, even for the girls.

The marches of John Philip Sousa were very popular and seemed to generate an excitement and raise patriotism. The Marine band, and often military music ensembles, were featured daily on the radio. All the children in the neighborhood knew, "You're a Grand Ole' Flag,"

"America the Beautiful," "My Country 'Tis of Thee," the National Anthem and "God Bless America." Kate Smith became a household name. To this day Marcia stands a little higher or sits up straighter when these and other American classics are played.

Marcia's father was the air raid warden for their precinct. He was medically deferred because of an earlier back injury. She remember sirens and blackouts and Daddy making sure the neighborhood was dark in the event of an enemy attack. She saw him as keeping them safe.

The Buck house was located only a short distance northwest of Wold-Chamberlain Field, now the Lindberg International Airport. It was an air force base during the war. As the little girls played outdoors, they dropped everything to watch those lumbering B-29 and B-17 bombers out on maneuvers. Marcia said, "I say lumbering now in retrospect and by today's standards of speed. To the normal kids on the street this was real speed."

Going to the local five-and-dime stores was something they would do after the Saturday matinee where they had just viewed the newsreels of the war in action. After Pearl Harbor, when they perused store shelves

Taught to pledge allegiance with hands extended, the Buck daughter grew patriotic right from birth and shared her training with her neighborhood friends. Left to right are Gail Russell, Marcia Buck, and Karen Russell. The flag they are pledging to is just off to the left.

The little girls on parade with their brooms and miscellaneous sticks and handles. Note the headpieces. From right to left they are: American Indian head dress, a sailor cap, and an infantry hat.

of glass figurines, they would pick them up, and look on the bottom. If the label had, "MADE IN JAPAN," they would declare them, "Jap junk," and put them back down. This was totally unacceptable in Marcia's home, prejudice wasn't allowed, not even towards the enemy.

The symbol for the Red Cross—the white flag with the red cross in the center—was practically sacred. Marcia knew the mission of the Red Cross was to help people. The little girls played Red Cross. They bandaged up their dolls, teddy bears and live cats after res-

Marcia and her friends imitating the patriotic bands.

cuing them from pretend battlefields. Once they were treated, they made meals for them as if from the Red Cross or the USO. They spent hours imitating the good deeds we knew the Red Cross performed.

"I have a hold over from World War II," Marcia relates. "It is recycling metal cans. I remove the labels and flatten the cans from force of habit, just as we did back in the days of war scrap drives."

Marcia's dad, as one of the few remaining men in our neighborhood, had a rather unusual job. After the GIs in the neighborhood had been home on leave, it was his duty to drive their wives to the hospital nine months later. He was not in attendance when either of his own daughters were born, however, because he was a salesman on the road.

One particular vivid memory Marcia has was of the V days. She was playing a couple blocks from home when suddenly the windows were opened on all the houses and some folks streamed out onto the front steps. Everyone was shouting, "The war is over! The war is over!" Marcia raced home to celebrate. She was so young, but loyalty and patriotism had been inculcated into her at a very early age.

After the war, things changed in the neighborhood. Veterans came home and put in applications for new housing. The suburb of Richfield started to develop. South of Minnehaha Creek was mostly country until after the war. Every vacant lot around the Bucks was purchased by a veteran. Marcia played with the neighborhood kids in the newly dug basements. When the construction workers would go home, they played in the newly framed houses. They went hand over hand on the floor joists. Marcia loved the smell of new wood. No one seemed worried about liability in those days, and Marcia does recall a broken or sprained ankle or two among the kids.

Schools had to expand quickly due to the influx of people. There must not have been enough money or supplies to build onto the school so railroad cars were moved to the school property for classroom space.

Life was changing rapidly. The kids tapered off playing war and Red Cross and then quit all together, though Marcia still has a special place in her heart for all she experienced as a child living in Minneapolis during World War II. "I will say this," Marcia said, "we found creative ways to play under all circumstances, rich or poor, war or peace."

Marcia married Richard Schut, and they live in Becker, Minnesota.

CELEBRATING V-E DAY AT THE GREYHOUND DEPOT - ST. CLOUD

Carol Wink Gross of St. Cloud has war-year memories relating to the bus depot. Carol is the daughter of Al and Genevieve Wink. They lived near Third Street and Thirty-Seventh Avenue North.

This family with six children—John, Norman, Donna, Norma, Eugene, and Carol—occasionally walked the nearly three miles to downtown St. Cloud. They enjoyed the bus depot when they saw travelers coming and going. Carol well remembers the sights, sounds, and even the smell of the exhaust from the buses that drove into the covered passenger-loading area. All this added much to the small world of the Gross family.

Carol's brothers John and Norman left to serve in the army during World War II. The family went to the bus depot to see them off.

Telegrams started arriving from the War Department concerning John. He was missing in action for a short time. Then a telegram came that said he was wounded. Carol was very young, but she recalled with clarity how often and how long her mother cried after each telegram arrived. After each such event, John returned to battle. He was a letter writer, but letters from soldiers were censored to hide specific locations and other sensitive information. They often had holes through the sentences that weren't allowed. Carol giggled about the holes poked through John's letters.

John was able to come home on a furlough, and the family rejoiced, but it ended too soon, and he had to return to his base. His leaving was terrible for the family. Several planned to wait with him at the bus depot. A neighbor, Amy Bettner, loaned the family her car so they didn't have to walk the three miles that time.

While they were waiting for John's bus on May 7, 1945, they heard a commotion out on St. Germain Street. Everyone in the depot went to see what was going on. Horns blared, church bells rang, and people were shouting. One man, in jubilation, rolled a car tire down the street. They learned that the Germans had surrendered. There was victory all over Europe. The *St. Cloud Daily Times* put out a special edition the next day, V-E Day.

What a relief for the Wink family! John still had to go to his base, but not back to battle. The mood of the family, even waiting for the bus to take their son away, had lifted. Carol was seven years old when both her brothers came home from the war.

Carol married Harland Gross, and they live in St. Cloud.

VERNA VORNBROCK GUETHER - ST. CLOUD

Verna lived with her family as a child in a strong German Catholic community west of St. Cloud in Stearns County. On Sunday, December 7, 1941, she walked to the bar, as the children did, to buy an ice cream cone. The bar radio was broadcasting the bombing of Pearl Harbor. Verna took her cone and ran home to tell her dad. He went to the bar to confirm this because they didn't have a radio at home. It was true.

As the United States entered the war, the priest had reason to believe this village could be headed for internment. German was the predominant language of the church, home, shops, and school. The priest insisted the church transition to English immediately. In school, the German-speaking children had to learn their handwriting terms and arithmetic in English and had to relearn their reading skills. It was a lot of work. In the business place, both shop owners and patrons practiced English and encouraged each other. Verna was fearful for years that her town would be taken to prison camp.

Internment camps for German-speaking people did not materialize for Verna or her town, but more than seventy internment camps existed in the United States during World War II under the Alien Enemies Act, and these include camps for Japanese, Germans, Italians, Hungarians, Romanians, Bulgarians, Czechs, and Poles. Some were in Minnesota. Fifty-six percent of all internees were Euopean-Americans. Over eleven thousand Germans were held. Verna and her town were indeed lucky.

JERRY SKELTON - ST. CLOUD

Jerry and his grandpa, Frank Moritz, heard that the government wanted to buy fur for collars on military jackets. They were told to trap the animals rather than shoot them because bullets tore through the hide, damaging the pelt.

Jerry and his grandpa trapped rabbits and other small animals in the Oak Park, Minnesota, area. They skinned the animals and dried the hides. When they had a wooden barrel full of pelts, they took it to a collection station and received the rate promised by the government, twelve dollars for a barrel of hides.

20

Post-War Memories

MARY BECHTOLD - LUXEMBURG, MINNESOTA

Immediately following the war, supplies remained in short supply for a time. Mary Bechtold (the younger sister of Rita Bechtold Recker) was the daughter of Lawrence and Hildegard Bechtold. She remembers that her First Communion was getting close, but she wanted a beautiful dress. Her mom ordered a used parachute, and it was delivered to their Luxemburg farm home. Hildegard then carefully sewed the slippery material

Mary Bechtold's Communion dress was made from a World War II used parachute in 1946. Shown are Mary's sponsors, Aunt Evelyn Klein and Uncle Wendelin Feneis.

on her non-electric treadle sewing machine powered by a foot pedal. Those machines required good hand, eye, and foot coordination, not made easier by the parachute fabric.

The Bechtold family had six boys and six girls. The parachute provided enough material for many dresses for the girls. They never had dresses from such elegant material before. Hildegard even figured out how to dye the cloth either pink or blue, which made the fabic nice for occasions other than First Communion. But Mary's special dress had a large ruffle sewn along the bottom, and she was very happy with the dress. A fabric created for war had been remade into something worn for a peaceful event.

The parachute fabric was kept in a wooden barrel. Some of the cords were still attached. Later, a mother cat crawled into the barrel to have a litter of kittens. That ended the parade of dresses made from the fabric. Mary Bechtold married Don Prom.

ARMY SURPLUS

Following the war, while civilian supplies remained low, there was a glut of army surplus clothing, equipment, and food. Army outlet stores began popping up in many places. In St. Cloud we had an outlet right downtown. Jack's Outlet became a favorite place for men to find field jackets and boots.

Many people purchased canvas army tents and set them up in their yards as kids' play tents. These tents had no floors. My dad bought two steel army beds and made them into bunk beds. They were brown and cost two dollars each. We used them for many years.

Charles "Bing" Skelton was in junior high school in St. Cloud at the end of the war. His parents were George and Barbara Moritz Skelton. Charles remembers that the junior high kids liked to get used gas mask bags and used them as school book bags. Real army steel helmets were something also sought after and shown off by kids.

Marge Waldorf Skelton, who attended a Catholic grade school in St. Cloud, said that army food rations turned up at her school and were served for lunch. Used to the privations of the Depression and World War II, people wasted nothing.

A Catholic nun at the St. Cloud Hospital told how excited her dad was to get a good buy on a new army jeep that had never left the country. He used it strictly on his farm in Luxemburg as a work vehicle pulling trailers and equipment around the farm. He never licensed it.

MOTHER LANDS A SECOND JOB

Though at the time I was dismayed, I am now amazed at my mother's courage to go out and apply for the job at the war plant during the war. She had married young and had many children and was otherwise always in the home. On top of that, she was incredibly shy. But that experience in the workplace gave her the boldness she needed to try for again for employment.

Two years after the war, she applied for a job as a cook at Lincoln Elementary, which was just a block from home. The hot lunch program was just being introduced, and she was free to serve whatever she wished to make. For the

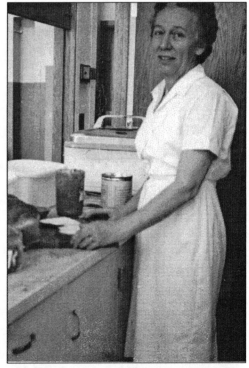

My mother landed a job as Rosie the Riveter during the war, then worked as a school cook for twenty-five years after the war in Lincoln Elementary School in St. Cloud.

113

next twenty-five years, she worked as a cook in the St. Cloud District #742 schools. She loved her job, and she made many friends among the staff and children.

TEMORARY HOUSING FOR RETURNING VETERANS

In 1946, following World War II, housing was needed in the United States for the returning veterans. Army bases had many empty trailer houses they no longer needed. About one hundred used army trailers were sent to St. Cloud and set up in two locations. One trailer park was on Thirty-Third Avenue North near Char Gale. The second one was on Eighth Street at about Twenty-Second Avenue North. They were named Trailer City One and Trailer City Two.

The trailers were rented out by rank with allowances made to those veterans with special needs. The trailer homes came in different sizes to accommodate families.

However, there were no bathrooms or even running water. One toilet and bath house trailer was set up for every nine trailer homes. Throughout the trailer park, utility trailers were stocked so renters could get pails for water and household use. After dishes, bathing and scrubbing were done, the waste water had to be carried to a utility trailer to be emptied. For laundry facilities, there were other trailers for common use, each supplied with a wringer washer, washtubs for rinsing, and clothes lines strung outside between poles for drying.

My sister Verna married Stanley Philipsek of St. Cloud when he returned from a stint in the army, serving in the Philippines. They rented a small trailer in the Eighth Street Park for sixteen dollars a month. I stayed with them occasionally. I thought it was great. I was fascinated by an English war bride who also lived in the park because of her accent. I also greatly enjoyed seeing the soldiers coming home and taking up residence in the parks. I needed to see these men who had been soldiers doing everyday things.

The army trailer houses as they are arriving in St. Cloud to house returning veterans. (Photo courtesy of the Stearns History Museum—Myron Hall Photo Collection)

This trailer is ready for skirting. (Photo courtesy of the Stearns History Museum—Myron Hall Photo Collection)

The trailers were not the greatest accommodations for the valiant military people coming home from war, but they weren't meant to be permanent. And few of the people in those trailers thought having no water was a terrible inconvenience. Most of the neighboring homes had yet to have running water or indoor toilet facilities either.

Women cleaning the rounded ceiling inside one of the army trailers. (Photo courtesy of the Stearns History Museum—Myron Hall Photo Collection)

Each camp had one officer on duty overseeing the activities in the park. A night guard monitored the park and grounds as well.

It cost a nickle to make a call from the free-standing phone booth in the park. Sometimes a line formed as people waited to make their calls. In the summer, this was a buggy wait, and it was cold in the winter. Tempers could flare if a caller talked too long.

I don't know how the trailers were heated because my sister and her husband bought a house before winter. As soon as people found other accommodations, they moved out, and the two trailer courts didn't stay up for long. My sister's husband, Stan, could have purchased a trailer for fifty dollars, but he didn't want one. Our grandfather, Herman Genz, bought one, however, and set it up on his property in Hayward Park, Minnesota. He rented it out for several years. During this phase, the soldiers were incorporated back into the community.

Conclusion

I am so grateful for each story shared by fellow Minnesotans who were children during World War II. It is time for us to be heard as we tell what we experienced on our young level. We lived and grew up while the war raged. We were together, not in space, but in purpose.

We worked in our Victory gardens and gathered cans for the scrap drives. At school we knitted afghans and bought war stamps We walked the countryside picking milkweed pods.

We feared the sound of planes overhead that might bomb us and huddled together in school basements when the air raid drill siren blew. During the newsreels of the war on the screen in the theatre, some of us shut our eyes and plugged our ears until it was over. Hitler scared us.

We knew our parents were worried when the mailman didn't bring letters, worried more that Western Union men would come. When parents talked of running out of rationing stamps, we caught that conversation and worried about that too. We knew what gold stars on the window flags meant. Children were not shielded from the realities of war, though many parents tried.

After all the work I did on this book and all the memories kicked up in the progress—my own and others'—I wanted a World War II keepsake made from a steel penny from the war years. The jeweler I went to, Dom Warzecha, immediately recognized the war coin. When I told him I was writing a book about the Minnesota children of World War II, he said, "Did you remember to write about the blackouts and the rationing stamps? How about the war stamps we bought?" We did some on-the-spot reminiscing. His wife, Eileen, was behind the counter too, her eyes a little teary, but she was smiling. She told of her family's celebration on the family farm just south of Cold Spring, Minnesota, when both of her brothers came home from foreign battlefields when the war was over. I will treasure the silver necklace even more knowing it was made by people who were part of the war years along with me.

Often over the years I thought of what I experienced during the war, but just never talked about it, not even to our children. I wrote many family historys, and the children know about their immigrant ancestors coming to America. And stories of World War II abound both in history and novel form. It's important that we remember what happened. But while the families at home did not place themselves in danger in the same way the soldiers did, the history of those times is not complete until the story at home has been told. What children experienced at home with a father, an older sibling, or other relative at war, adds to the history of World War II. It is time to relate these stories before this piece of history is lost.

This collection of stories that I have gathered and written have a place in World War II memories. The picture is more complete, when the children left at home, speak out on how families functioned on the home front. Their meaningful remembrances add to the stories of war.

I am proud that I was a Minnesota child of World War II.

ABOUT THE AUTHOR

Sharon Eberhardt Schulte lives in St. Cloud, Minnesota, with her husband, Tom. They celebrated their fiftieth wedding anniversary in 2005. Five children were born to them, all raised in St. Cloud and all still in the area.

Sharon is a free-lance writer and has been published on local, state and national levels, writing on a variety of topics. For a time, she was an at-home joke writer for the nationally known comedienne Phyllis Diller. Over the years, she has had the pleasure of sharing her writing skills in composing letters for family and friends challenged by a situation where a letter will assist them. She considers it a privilege to share. A young girl in a beauty pageant didn't have a talent to exhibit, so Sharon wrote a humorous essay for her to read.

Long Minnesota winters gave Sharon time to write a book about the family hobby, stock car racing in Minnesota (unpublished). She honors her long life and has written extensively about the senior citizens in the family.

Their firstborn child, Sandra, has Down's Syndrome, functions at a four-year-old level and has always lived at home. When Sandy became an aunt to her siblings' children, Sharon wrote a book entitled, *Aunt Sandy*.

Now she has kept a promise to herself to write a book about what she and other Minnesota children experienced during World War II. She and her publisher are both pleased she kept this promise.

ACKNOWLEDGEMENTS

I want to express my sincere thanks to all of those people who willing shared their childhood memories of what they experienced in Minnesota during World War II.

I had an incredible support team. My sister, Verna Eberhardt Phiilipsek, plus our cousin, LaVon Eberhardt Kedrowski, who lived in the neighborhood when we were children, were always available to me to help me focus in on a situation. They both still live in the area. Being as they are some years older than I, they added detail to my writings.

My grade-school friend, Sibyl Stark Pelz did research for me and spoke encouraging words as often as I needed them. She helped me get to the finish line. Time and again, Marge and Waldorf Skelton added meaningful insights to the book.

Nancy Fitch and Rita Reker, who have been my close friends for forty years, supported me by adding pictures and colorful memories.

I enrolled in a class taught by Seal Dwyer at the Whitney Senior Center in St. Cloud, Minnesota, entitled "How to Get Your Book Published." Her teachings helped me to go above and beyond what I thought was possible.

The work of the staff at Stearns Heritage Museum, John Decker, Bob Lommel, and Sara LaVine, located pictures and facts that gave depth to my stories.

At home my husband, Tom, and our four adult children, when they stopped by, were ever so patient with me. I told and re-told every story as I collected it. They were good listeners as I related from my heart the deep stories.

My granddaughter, Sara, did some art work for me.

All these people made it possible for me to share the memories of Minnesota children during World War II.